The Topeka Outpouring of 1901:

Eyewitness Accounts of the Revival that Birthed the 20th Century Pentecostal/Charismatic Movements

Compiled and Edited by
Larry Martin

 Christian Life Books
Joplin, Missouri 64803

*For information on other books on Pentecostal\Charismatic
history, please write:*
Christian Life Books
P.O. Box 2152
Joplin, Missouri 64803

Dedication

I am dedicating this work to my sweetheart, Tajuana Jo Martin. She has always been a trusted friend, faithful wife and loving mother. Now, more than ever, she is my partner in the pursuit of Pentecostal revival.

Contents

Acknowledgments

A special thanks goes to Aaron Wilson for the use of his computer and his expertise. Aaron, you are one of God's most generous servants. You and Marthel are in our prayers.

Thanks to Doug Gilmore for help with the cover and to Brian Ramos for overseeing the production of the book. Your friendship is appreciated.

David Coleman, one of my former students at Messenger College, painted the water color for the front cover. Thank you, David, your work is always excellent.

I owe a deep debt of gratitude to these guardians of our heritage: the Assemblies of God Archives, the Kansas State Historical Society and the Apostolic Faith Report. The historical materials found in this book would not be available except for their tireless work.

Thanks to my friend, Rev. Warren Harkins, for inviting me to revivals in Miami and Pensecola. My deepest appreciation goes to Evangelist John Davis, Pastor Gerald Baser and the excited people at First Assembly of God in Miami, Oklahoma for reminding me that the days of God's visitation are not over. The best is yet to come.

8

Preface

The Twentieth Century Pentecostal/Charismatic revival has proven to be one of the greatest spiritual awakenings since the Day of Pentecost. Many have compared the revival with the Reformation initiated by Martin Luther in the Sixteenth Century.

Estimates of the number of Pentecostals and Charismatics in the world today have reached as high as one-half billion. If this estimate is correct, Pentecostalism is the largest doctrinal body within the Protestant Christian faith. These numbers are especially remarkable considering the movement is less than one hundred years old and began in such humble circumstances.

Those who have studied the Pentecostal Revival know that the distinctive doctrine of the faith (tongues speaking as the initial physical evidence of the Holy Spirit baptism) was first articulated near the turn of the century at Bethel Bible College in Topeka, Kansas. Despite some claims to the contrary, Charles Fox Parham, the founder and administrator of that college, is undeniably the father of modern Pentecostalism.

In his excellent work on the life of Parham, James R. Goff, Jr. says, "It was Parham who first formulated the theological definition of Pentecostalism by linking tongues with the Holy Spirit baptism."

I am releasing this collection of eyewitness accounts of the miraculous Topeka outpouring, as the one-hundredth anniversary of the event draws near. The passing generation must never forget this great episode and a new generation should be able to share in the story of the birth of Pentecost.

Most of these accounts have been published before, but never in this format. Many have been out of print for decades. I am including a brief biography of Parham and a number of never published photographs.

As you read, you will notice minor variations and contradictions in the stories. This should not be surprising. As with witnesses to any event, different people will have a slightly different view or memory of the occurrence. If four people standing on each corner of an intersection viewed an automobile accident, each would describe the crash from their own perspective. Please do not let these minor contradictions be a stumbling block. The most important thing is that these marvelous events did occur and they started a mighty revival that has swept the world.

On January 22, 1901, as Parham and his band of followers left on a missionary trip to Kansas City and beyond, a reporter for the **Topeka Daily Capital** wrote,"It is not improbable that Topeka has heard the last about the college and the strange gift its students were miraculouly given."

How could anyone be so wrong? Neither Topeka, nor the world has heard the last of Parham and the wonderful gift of tongues.

I pray that you will be blessed by this exciting story of a Holy Ghost outpouring that continues to change the world.

Larry Martin
Christian Life Books

Charles F. Parham
From **The Life of Charles F. Parham**
(Public Domain)

Sarah E. Parham
From **The Life of Charles F. Parham**
(Public Domain)

The William Parham Family
Charles F., Harry, Baby Arthur, William, Edward and
Frank
Apostolic Faith Report
(Used by Permission)

Charles F. Parham Tent Revival
Apostolic Faith Report
(Used by Permission)

Chapter 1

CHARLEſ FOX PARHAM: FATHER OF THE TWENTIETH CENTURY PENTECOſTAL REVIVAL

By Larry E. Martin

This book is a historical record of the events that took place in Topeka, Kansas almost one hundred years ago. It is about an episode that has changed the history of the church. This book is also about a man, Charles F. Parham. It was under his leadership that the Pentecostal\Charismatic movement began. No single individual was more important to the birth and initial growth of the movement than Parham.

Parham was born June 4, 1873 in Muscatine County, Iowa.[1] When he was five, his family moved to Kansas where Parham spent most of his life. As a child, Parham experienced many debilitating illnesses including encephalitis and rheumatic fever.[2] These unfortunate confrontations with pain, and even death, would greatly impact his adult life.

Even before his conversion at age thirteen, Parham felt an attraction to the Bible and a call to preach. He began conducting revival meetings in local Methodist churches when he was fifteen.[3] In 1890 he started his formal ministerial training at Southwest Kansas College.[4]

A year later Parham turned his back on God and the ministry. Deciding that he preferred the income and social standing of a physician, he began medical studies.[5] Soon his rheumatic fever returned and it didn't seem that Parham would recover.[6] He trusted God for his healing, and the pain and fever that had tortured his body for months immediately disappeared. However, the healing was not yet complete. Months of inactivity had left Parham a virtual cripple. His ankles were too weak to support the weight of his body so he staggered about walking on the sides of his feet. In December 1891, Parham renewed his commitments to God and the ministry and he was instantaneously and totally healed.[7]

Parham served a brief term as a Methodist pastor, but left the organization after a falling out with his ecclesiastical superiors.[8] He then became loosely affiliated with the holiness movement that split from the Methodists late in the Nineteenth Century. He never returned to structured denominationalism.

On December 31, 1896, Parham married Sarah Eleanor Thistlethwaite, a devoted Quaker.[9] The young couple worked together in the ministry, conducting revival campaigns in several Kansas cities. Influenced by a number of successful faith healers, Parham's holiness message evolved to include an ever increasing emphasis on divine healing. Eventually, Parham arrived at the belief that the use of medicines was forbidden in the Bible.[10]

In the summer of 1898, the aspiring evangelist moved his family to Topeka and opened Bethel Healing Home. For almost two years, the home served both the physical and spiritual needs of the city. Included in the services that Parham offered were an infirmary, a Bible Institute, an adoption agency, and even an unemployment office. Parham also published a religious periodical, **The**

15

Apostolic Faith. In only a few years, this would become the world's first Pentecostal journal.[11]

After suffering a nervous breakdown in September 1899, Parham entered a period of study and persona introspection. He considered the theological positions of John Alexander Dowie, A.B. Simpson, Benjamin Hardin Irwin and others as he molded his own religious belief.[12]

In the Summer of 1900, Parham took a sabbatical from the healing home to embark on a spiritual odyssey throughout the Northeastern United States. For three months he visited some of the most prominent ministries in the nations. None had a greater impact on his theology than Frank W. Sanford of Durham, Maine.[13]

Like all Wesleyan Holiness believers, Parham taught that sanctifications was a second work of God's grace. But, when he was introduced to Sanford's teaching and the Fire-Baptized Holiness movement, he began to enlarge his theology to include an experience beyond sanctification. This "third blessing," as Parham began to understand it was a personal baptism in the Holy Spirit, identical to that which the Church Fathers received in the second chapter of Acts. This baptism, Parham believed, would empower Christians for the last-days harvest of souls.

When the preacher returned to Topeka early in the fall of 1900, he found that the colleagues he had left in charge of the haling home had staged a religious *coup d'etat* gaining control of the facility.[14] Not deterred by their disloyalty, in October, Parham relocated to an elaborate fifteen room house in Topeka. The financial misfortunes of the builder led local residents to give the castle-like structure the dubious nickname "Stone's Folly." With thirty-four students, Parham began Bethel Bible College, a Bible school that would emphasize the Holy Spirit Baptism.[15] Parham was especially interested in the way the experience related to missionary activities.

Parham said, "Our purpose in this Bible School was not to learn things in our head only but have each thing in the Scriptures wrought out in our hearts."[16] All students (mostly mature, seasoned gospel workers) were expected to sell everything they owned and give the proceeds away so each could trust God for daily provisions. From this humble college, a theology was developed that would change the face of the Christian church forever.

After a study of the book of Acts, the students entered a time of prayer and waiting on God. On January 1, 1901, Agnes Nevada Ozman, a thirty-year old student, received the Baptism in the Holy Ghost with the evidence of speaking in a language she did not know (known as glossolalia).[17] In the days following, Parham and a number of other students received the experience and spoke with tongues.

Most church historians agree that the episode at Stone's Mansion initiated the modern Pentecostal revival. In less than a century the Breath of God would spread the flames of Pentecost like a windswept fire from the Kansas prairies to the uttermost parts of the earth.

This is not to suggest that this was the first modern incident of tongues speaking. In fact, from the time of the Apostles until today there have been occasions when believers, caught up in the Spirit, spoke in tongues. The Huguenots in France and Irvingites in England both shared the experience. The great revivals of Wesley, Finney and Moody were sometimes accompanied by manifestations of spiritual gifts.[18]

By the latter Nineteenth Century there had been numerous occurrences of speaking in tongues. Confirmed reports came from Minnesota, North Carolina, Texas and Tennessee in the decade before Parham's group received their Baptism in the Holy Ghost.

Yet, the experience at Bethel College was unique. Parham and his students reached the theological conclusion that speaking in other tongues was the scriptural evidence of the Holy Spirit Baptism. Earlier, tongues had been viewed as a demonstration of the Spirit similar to weeping, shouting, or shaking. Parham's group received the Baptism with evidential tongues while earnestly seeking the experience.[19] Unlike his predecessors, Parham taught that those who did not speak in tongues had never received the fullness of the Holy Spirit.

The young preacher soon accompanied a team of evangelists who went forth from Topeka to share what Parham called the "Apostolic Faith" message. Unfortunately, their earliest attempts at spreading the news were less than successful. After the tragic death of Parham's youngest child, Bethel College closed and Parham entered another period of introspection. During this time he wrote and published the first book of Pentecostal theology, **Kol Kare Bomidbar: A Voice Crying in the Wilderness**.[20]

Parham's first successful Pentecostal meetings were in Galena and Baxter Springs, Kansas and Joplin, Missouri in 1903 and 1904. Hundreds were saved, healed and baptized in the Holy Spirit as Parham preached to thousands in the booming mine towns.[21]

Following the fruitful meetings in Kansas and Missouri, Parham set his eyes on the Lone Star State. In the spring and summer of 1905 the evangelist conducted a highly successful crusade in Orchard, Texas, and then he moved his team to the Houston-Galveston area. After returning to Kansas for a few months, he moved his entire enterprise to Houston and opened another Bible College. "The Bible Training School", as it was called, provided ten weeks of intensive Pentecostal indoctrination.[22]

William Joseph Seymour, a Black holiness evangelist, became one of Parham's early students. Because Parham was a strict segregationist, Seymour was not allowed in the room with the white brethren. Parham, nevertheless, accommodated him by leaving the door open so that he could hear the Apostolic Faith message from the hallway.[23] After only five weeks in Parham's classes, Seymour received a call to pastor in Los Angeles, California. At first Parham discouraged him from leaving, but eventually helped him raise money for the journey west.[24] Even though he had not received the Baptism in the Holy Ghost, Seymour was convinced of the reality of this "third blessing."

Within months, Seymour had opened the Azusa Street Mission in Los Angeles and the West Coast became the center for the Pentecostal revival. Hundreds accepted the Full Gospel message at the dilapidated mission. When Parham visited California in the fall of 1906, he condemned the excessive emotionalism and mixing of the races prevalent in the services. After Seymour introduced Parham as his "father in the Gospel of the Kingdom," the latter responded, "God is sick at His stomach!"[25] The first Pentecostal theologian rejected all fleshly manifestations of emotion and refused to be connected with "Holy Rollers."

The California brethren, stung by Parham's denunciations, rejected the self proclaimed "Founder and Projector of the Apostolic Faith." The movement that Parham had founded was already outgrowing the leadership of the young Kansan.

Parham continued to travel across the United States holding revivals and sharing the full gospel message. He even fulfilled a lifetime dream by making a trip to the Holy Land.

Yet, when he died in Baxter Springs, Kansas on January 29, 1929, Parham no longer held significant influence over the movement he had started less than three decades earlier. In fact, the earliest Pentecostal historians often ignored his contribution to the movement.

Several important factors contributed to his swift decline in popular support. Chief among these were reports of sexual misconduct. Although he vehemently denied any wrongdoing and hard evidence of immorality does not exist, these rumors followed him much of his life.[26]

Yet, it was more than gossip and innuendo that spelled the end of Parham's influence. The movement as a whole refused to embrace Parham's more extreme doctrines. For example, he taught the total annihilation of the wicked, a view rejected by all other Pentecostals.[27] Parham believed that Christians who did not receive the Baptism in the Holy Spirit, confirmed by tongues, would not be "sealed" for the Marriage Supper of the Lamb.[28]

Parham also believed that tongues speaking was not the authentic evidence of the Holy Spirit Baptism unless it was xenoglossic (a known human language). Early in his career, he believed that God would send forth Spirit filled, tongue talking missionaries who would not have to learn foreign languages to evangelize the world.[29]

Certainly, Parham's racist views are more disturbing today than they were almost a century ago, but even for that time they must have been shocking to some followers. He is accused of telling blacks that they could not become part of the Bride of Christ because of their race.[30] He also believed that interracial marriages caused the flood of Noah.[31] His teachings on white superiority also included Anglo-Israelism, a cultic doctrine which argues that Anglo-Saxons are the ten lost tribes of Israel.[32] Parham "associated freely and often" with the Ku Klux Klan.[33]

More than any of this, perhaps, it was Parham's disdain for denominational organization that prevented him from becoming the most prominent leader of the Apostolic Faith or Pentecostal movement. By the time of his death, most Pentecostal groups were well organized and prospering while Parham, his ministry floundering, continued to preach against organization. In a very real sense, the death of his influence came from self-inflicted wounds.

Nevertheless, Parham will never be forgotten. He was the first modern Pentecostal theologian, he wrote the first Pentecostal book, and he published the first Pentecostal magazine.

Despite his obvious shortcomings, Charles Fox Parham should and will be remembered and respected as the founder of the Twentieth Century Pentecostal revival.

NOTES

[1]James R. Goff, *Fields White Unto Harvest: Charles F. Parham and the Missionary Origins of Pentecostalism* (Fayetteville: U of Arkansas, 1988), 18.

[2]Stanley M. Burgess and Gary B. McGee, eds, *Dictionary of Pentecostal and Charismatic Movements* (Grand Rapids: Zondervan, 1988), 660.

[3]Goff, 27.

[4]Burgess, 660.

[5]Goff, 28.

[6]*Ibid*, 28-29.

[7]*Ibid.*, 29.

[8]Robert M. Anderson, *Vision of the Disinherited: The Making of American Pentecostalism* (Peabody: Hendrickson, 1979), 49.

[9]Goff, 38.

[10]*Ibid.*, 39.

[11]*Ibid.*, 41-46.

[12]*Ibid.*, 49-56.

[13]Burgess, 660

[14] Gordon Lindsey, *They Saw It Happen: The Dramatic Story of Men of God Who Were Greatly Used in the Pentecostal Outpouring of the Twentieth Century* (Dallas: Christ for the Nations, 1983), 14.

[15]Goff, 61-65.

[16]Charles F. Parham and Sarah E. Parham, *Selected Sermons of the Late Charles F. Parham and Sarah E. Parham* (Baxter Springs: Apostolic Faith Bible College, n.d), 75.

[17]There are conflicting stories about exactly how and when Agnes Ozman received the Holy Ghost Baptism. The reader shold study the following chapters and draw his or her own conclusion.

[18]These experiences are well documented. See Carl Brumback, *What Meaneth This?: A Pentecostal Answer to A Pentecostal Question*, (Springfield: Gospel, 1947), 89-96.

[19]Klaude Kendrick, *The Promise Fulfilled: A History of the Modern Pentecostal Movement.* (Springfield: Gospel Publishing, 1961), 53.

[20]Goff, 83-86.

[21]*Ibid.*, 87-94.

[22]Vinson Synan, *The Holiness-Pentecostal Movement in the United States.*, (Grand Rapids: Eerdmans, 1971), 103.

[23]Iain MacRobert, *The Black Roots and White Racism of Early Pentecostalism in the U.S.A.* (New York: St. Martin's, 1988), 51.

[24]Goff, 111.

[25]*The Apostolic Faith,* May 1921, 6 and Goff, 129-131.

[26]The fact that Parham was arrested and charged with sodomy has been well documented. Parham and his followers denied the allegations and accused enemies in Zion City, Illinois of framing the evangelist. See Goff, 136-140.

[27]Charles F. Parham, *The Everlasting Gospel* (Baxter Spings: Apostolic Faith Bible College, n.d.), 111-117.

[28]Edith L. Blumhoffer, *The Assemblies of God: A Chapter in the Story of American Pentecostalism, vol. 1* (Springfield: Gospel Publishing, 1989), 74.

[29]Goff, 72, 154.

[30]*The Apostolic Faith,* May 1921, 6.

[31]*Gospel of the Kingdom,* April 1910, 1.

[32]Charles F. Parham, *Kol Kare Bomidbar: A Voice Crying in the Wilderness* Baxter Spings: Apostolic Faith   Bible College, n.d.), 105-108.

[33]James L. Tyson, *The Early Pentecostal Revival: History of Twentieth-Century Pentecostals and the Pentecostal Assemblies of the World, 1901-1930* Hazelwood: Word Aflame, 1992), 73.

This chapter is a revision of an article which originally appeared in Dr. Martin's book, **In the Beginning***, published by Christian Life Books in 1994.*

Charles F. Parham   Agnes N. Ozman

Both sketches from **The Topeka Journal**
January 9, 1901
(Public Domain)

Charles F. Parham in his office.
Apostolic Faith Report
(Used by Permission)

Chapter 2

BETHEL HEALING HOME

By Sarah E. Parham

In 1898, we established a Divine Healing Home on the corner of Fourth and Jackson Streets, Topeka, Kansas, which we called, "Bethel." It was a nice brick building centrally located and had all modern conveniences.

From the outside, the building looks very much the same now, but it may have been remodeled inside. The ground floor furnished a large chapel, public reading room and printing office. The second floor had fourteen rooms, and we kept the large windows in the parlors filled with flowers, as Mr. Parham was a great lover of flowers and we wanted to make the rooms look cheerful to the sick. The third floor was simply an attic, but we used it for sleeping purposes when our bed rooms were all occupied.

The purpose of the Bethel Home was to provide homelike comforts for those who were seeking healing, while we prayed for their spiritual needs as well as their bodies. We also found Christian homes for orphan children, and work for the unemployed.

Our paper, **The Apostolic Faith**, was published twice a month. At first we had a subscription price, later we announced for subscription price see, Isaiah 55:1 and the Lord wonderfully provided. Each number of the paper was filled with wonderful testimonies to healing and sermons containing the teachings of the home.

Special studies were given to ministers and evangelists, and many workers were instructed in Bible truths, and trained for gospel work. We taught salvation, healing, sanctification, the second coming of Christ, and the baptism of the Holy Spirit, although we had not then received the evidence of speaking in other tongues, as we did later in the "College of Bethel."

We practiced water baptism by immersion, and partook of the Lord's supper. Being raised in the Friend's Church, I had not been taught the importance of this ordinance, but God so wonderfully blessed us as we partook of the bread and the wine that I found it a sacred privilege to "do this in remembrance of Him." These services were a great blessing to the guests in the home, and one of them gave the following report, "A feast of fat things was enjoyed by the brothers and sisters Sunday night in the parlors of the home when they partook of the Lord's supper, followed by the sacrament. The praise and thanksgiving of many pure hearts ascended to God as they let their thoughts run back through the ages to the time when Jesus sat down thus with His disciples, and many felt His Presence. Earnest thought was given by each one as to whether, since we last met, any had played the part of Judas in betraying our Lord. It was an inspiration to see the happy expectant faces and eyes filled with tears of joy as the word was passed down the table that it wouldn't be very long until we would sit thus with Him in His Kingdom.

"Before passing, the bread and wine, Brother Parham, gave some convincing thoughts, showing definitely that healing was in the atonement. Taking up the thought of the Passover Lamb, both the body and the blood had their designed purpose: in taking in the sacrifices that typified

Christ, the body as well as the blood had some definite purpose of atonement. While the blood was for the cleansing of the sin, His perfect body was broken for our imperfect bodies; that is, to bring us to perfect health. With His stripes we are healed."

Now, I will quote from others that have written about the home which will give you some idea of the work that Mr. Parham was doing at that time, "This blessed Sabbath morning, this morning of all mornings, I am carried away in thought and in spirit from earth to higher thoughts. While sitting in the private office of the 'Apostolic Faith' these beautiful lines come to me, 'By their fruits ye shall know them.' What are the fruits of Bethel? I was a stranger and they took me in; I was an hungered and they gave me to eat; was athirst, and they gave me to drink; was weary and they gave me a bed, without price, and more precious than all, gave me spiritual food that is digestible, that though a person be ever so unlearned, he can understand. I know that God is going to answer my prayer, I know I am going to be healed.

"Bethel is all that name implies, and more, and to be appreciated must be seen. It is certainly a fulfillment of the Scriptures, where we can come together though we be strangers, yet feel the assurance that we are welcome; where everyone is a brother and sister in deed and in truth. God will surely bless Brother and Sister Parham in their endeavor to build up His Kingdom upon earth. They are not waiting until we are placed beneath the earth that we may enjoy some of the foretaste of heaven upon earth, but that God's kingdom can be established here in man's heart, where all can dwell together in peace and love, for perfect love casteth out fear."

Another writes, "As I have been a guest at Bethel, I feel impressed to write something concerning the home and its work. Who could think of a sweeter name than 'Bethel?' Surely it is none other than the House of God. Everything moves in love and harmony. On entering the rooms one is impressed with the divine influence shed abroad there. Here is a place where the sin-sick soul may come and be taught the way of salvation and a higher life; also where those who are sick may be taught that it is 'God who healeth all our diseases and redeemeth our life from destruction' (Psalm 103:3-4).

"It is a faith home all the way through. Brother Parham and his coworkers are heart and soul consecrated to the work of God. They live by faith believing that "my God shall supply all your needs according to His riches in glory by Christ Jesus," and truly God does verify His promise to them. I have been afflicted for years with various diseases, today I am rejoicing in a Savior that keeps me, soul and body. I also received such an uplift spiritually, and the Bible is a new book to me. Praise God for such a Home."

Eva Baker wrote, "To some of us who are looking to the dawn of that bright day when the Son of Righteousness shall rise with 'healing in His wings' and usher in His reign of peace and love, there seems a foretaste of the spirit of it, in this 'House of God.' A stranger coming among the little company of believers assembled here, cannot but feel here is a Christian home in the highest sense of the word.

"To the comforts and informality of home life, is added that spirit of cheerfulness and consideration for others which reveals the Christ life within seeking earnestly to realize that ideal life, being a bond of union to draw together a little community who see the necessity of living for the highest ends.

"God has wonderfully answered the prayers of His faithful followers; prayers that rise continually from all hearts. Here the sick are healed, souls are saved, and rich and poor have the gospel preached to them. May God bless this noble work, dedicated to suffering humanity; and deeply bless also the devoted pastor, C. F. Parham, and his coworkers."

An elderly lady, Mrs. Ellen Tanner, was wonderfully healed in the Home and remained with us for some time. Her sweet Christian life was a benediction, and she was like a real mother to us all. In her testimony, she often praised God that "He was not dead or gone on a journey," and how wonderfully we felt His living presence and power with us as she testified.

She wrote the following account May 3, 1899, of Easter Sunday at Bethel, "The first sound heard on this sacred Sabbath, was the singing of 'Sweet Hour of Prayer' by Brother Parham. This as usual assembled the household in one of the front parlors for worship, which is always a season of refreshing. A chapter of the Word was read and explained by Brother Parham in the most helpful manner, applying the Scriptures to our daily needs and lives. Our prayers were supplemented by two brothers one having come to bring his invalid daughter whose life was despaired of, that she might be taught how to receive divine healing; the other for a little physical and much spiritual help.

"After we had partaken of an excellent breakfast with joyful thanksgiving, one of the sisters visited an invalid in her room, and fervent prayer was offered that the Holy Spirit might come in and abide with her.

"The morning service was a suitable memorial of the day on which Christ arose from the dead; and the story as told by the beloved disciple was read and accepted as the ground of our hope of a resurrection and immortal life. The pastor's subject was the earnest desire of Paul to know Christ and the power of His resurrection. He set forth the blessed truth, that we were not to stop at knowing Christ on the cross, but were to follow on and know the Lord in His resurrection. To know Him as our chosen One, as Christ within us, with love, joy, peace and righteousness, health and strength, sufficient for all believers who will reach up with the arm of faith to bring down His riches in glory.

"The invalid and her father, not knowing that divine strength had been asked for, were astonished that she was able to sit through the services of the day without fatigue.

"The gospel of healing is usually taught after the 2 P. M. Sunday School, but this Easter Sunday we listened to the gospel of love that casteth out fear--fear of death; fear of the assaults of our enemies; fear that God's divine power will not be sufficient for us under all circumstances. The love that Christ felt for all mankind, His enemies included; love that would mold all of God's dear people into His own image, and cement them together as one body in Christ Jesus, so that His last prayer might be fulfilled--that we might be one even as He and the Father were one. The preacher insisted that God would work mightily in answer to prayer, where so many agreed 'as touching one thing' either as regards the salvation of the sinner or the healing of the sick body.

"An altar service was held at the close of the service. Several sisters claimed healing, which is 'the children's bread.' God's presence was manifested in great power and the healing work was done. The cordial greetings always extended to the strangers and friends being over, the hall was deserted, except for a few who remained for the evening meeting.

"There had been a desire on the part of some of the best supporters of the mission to organize, elect a board for the supervision of the finances, etc., and pay the pastor a stated salary. But the pastor having accepted Apostolic faith, petitioned God most earnestly that He would set the divine seal of approval upon the work by providing the means to pay the month's rent on the building. The prayer was answered--the rent was forth coming and thirteen dollars beside.

"The night service was a blessed meeting, Jesus Himself being in the midst and confirming the Word by signs following. Two sisters testified to having been healed at Bethel that afternoon. One lady went forward, confessed her sins and was accepted of God. Three others sought the healing touch. This was one typical Sabbath in this home of prayer.

"The family life was an earnest of heaven. Mrs. Parham and her sister [Lilian Thistlethwaite. *Ed.*] are of

English Quaker origin. They are gentle, peaceful, unselfish, thinking only of the comfort and welfare of their guests. The babies of Bethel are truly 'things of beauty and joys forever.'

"The doctrine is that of holiness with the 'I am holier than thou' left out; of healing in answer to prayer after a complete consecration of our lives and our all to God; peace with God and all mankind. It is often necessary to explain that he who lays hands on you and prays for your healing is no more a divine healer than he who prays for your salvation from sin, is a savior. It is God who does the work in both instances in answer to prayer.

"The mighty power of God as revealed in answered prayer, made the world to recede and a light as from heaven shone about me and led me to inquire, 'What kind of a world is this you have here, with God taking such active part in all your affairs?'

"One night while listening to the testimonies of God's miraculous healing, I was for an instant carried back to the days of the first disciples. I was in Samaria attending Philip's revival. Peter and John had been sent down from Jerusalem, and the power of the Holy Ghost had fallen upon the people. Going back to the Apostolic faith, we find ourselves in a new world. The days of miracles are repeated. 'The prayer of faith shall save the sick and the Lord shall raise him up;' and best of all, 'if he hath committed sins they be forgiven him.'"

Another resident wrote, "The work that is being done here cannot be estimated. It is a house of prayer, and the influence is felt on coming in the rooms. Hardly a day passes that some one does not come for prayer for their healing, and some days there are many. Consumptives, dyspeptics, cripples, and people with almost every known disease come for healing, and the best part of it all is that those that come for healing always get a spiritual uplift, such as they never knew before. It would be a miserable mortal indeed who would not praise the Lord after being healed by His wonderful power.

"We have been boarding in the home about six weeks, and we have failed to discover anything that is not of God in the life of the occupants. Everything moves in peace and harmony; and love prevails everywhere. I consider myself greatly privileged to be here. The power of God is here, the peace that passeth understanding, and the perfect love that casteth out fear pervades the very atmosphere of the place. Praise the Lord, there is such a place in Kansas, or on earth, in the midst of these dreadful times of doubt and skepticism. My boy has been healed twice since coming here, once of a very bad cold and once of a very bad attack of tonsillitis."

Charles Parham, himself, describes the work as follows, "Once after returning from a hard day's labor among the sick from the death bed of the president of the Santa Fe Railroad, it being a few minutes past 11 o'clock, the fact was suddenly flashed into my mind that the next day the rent was due, with not a cent to meet it. Tired and weary, I looked into the starlit sky, saying, 'Father, this is Thy part of the work, I must have rest and sleep tonight, Thou hast never failed us, Thou wilt not now.'

"Next morning before we had risen, there came a knock at the door. Quickly throwing on a dressing robe, I answered the call. An Eastern gentleman, who was visiting in the city, and knew something of our work among the poor and needy in the city, greeted me with a cheery, 'Good morning,' then saying. 'Last night, between eleven and twelve o'clock (being the hour that I had prayed) I was suddenly awaken with the thought of you and your work; no sleep came to me until I had promised to bring you this.' Handing me a slip of paper, he said, 'I bring you St. Patrick's greetings.' He lifted his hat and was gone. On entering the parlor, I examined the paper at the window and found it to be a check for forty dollars, the exact sum of our rent.

"At another time when a bill of seventy-five dollars was due, I arose in the morning with but twenty-five to meet it with. Asking God's blessing upon this sum that He would increase it, I passed on to the bank, which was situated in the center of the block. I was crossing the street, when a gentleman hailed me, saying, 'I am so very glad to see you. We sold one of our farms yesterday, and as we always give a tenth, reserved this sum for you.' He handed me a slip of paper. Not looking at its sum, (a practice I always follow) I thanked him for it, and entered the bank, where with pleasure and gratitude I discovered it to be a check for fifty dollars. With the twenty-five already in my possession, it made up the seventy-five due that morning.

"It made no difference whether our monthly expense amounted to a few or hundreds of dollars, just that sum was at hand to meet the demands, never having anything extra with which to become proud or puffed up and forget the origin of our help. 'He is faithful who has promised.'"

March 1, 1900, a new guest entered our home, a fine brown-eyed baby boy, our second son. We named him Charles for his father. Soon after this a parsonage was provided for us which was more convenient, and we were glad the children could have a lawn for a play ground.

Some evangelists from the east held a few days meeting for us, as our work was undenominational and our mission doors ever open to all who preached the gospel. Our hearts were stirred to deepen our consecration, and to "search the Word."

Concerning the last days of the healing home, Mr. Parham wrote, "Deciding to know more fully the latest truths restored by latter day movements, I left my work in charge of two Holiness preachers and visited various movements, such as Dowie's work who was then in Chicago; the Eye-Opener work of the same city; Malone's work in Cleveland, Dr. Simpson's work in Nyack, New York, Sanford's 'Holy Ghost and Us' work at Shiloah, Maine, and many others.

"I returned home fully convinced that while many had obtained real experience in sanctification and the anointing that abideth, there still remained a great outpouring of power for the Christians who were to close this age.

"Through underhanded scheming and falsehoods, the ministers I left in charge of my work had not only taken my building but most of my congregation. My friends urged me to claim my own, but the Word says, 'We have heard that it hath been said, An eye for an eye, and a tooth for a tooth: But I say unto you, That ye resist not evil; but whosoever smite thee on thy right cheek, turn to him the other also, and if any man will sue thee at the law, and take away thy coat, let him have thy cloak also.' To practice His Word was our highest aim.

"God in a marvelous way had provided for my family during my absence. Though friends may fail, God is ever faithful and had put it in the hearts of His children in different towns and states, to supply their needs. One day, when there was nothing to eat in the house, the table was set for supper looking for God to supply. Then came a knock at the door, and there stood a lady with a big basket in her hand. Though she had never been to the house before, she explained that she felt that she should fix supper for them, as my wife had done a big washing, and hoped it would be accepted. The big washing was not an unusual thing, as beside her own she did the washing for the poor sick ones at the healing home, desiring to help them all she could. Our neighbor didn't realize it was God who had put it in her heart to supply the need at the right time. Here was supper all cooked, ready to set on the table.

"Then came a stranger who had gone to the post office to mail his tithes to foreign fields, but felt led to bring it to my wife instead. It is more blessed to give than to receive and he received a great blessing as he realized how wonderfully God had led him.

"I went to my room to fast and pray, to be alone with God that I might know His will for my future work. Many of my friends desired me to open a Bible School. By a series of wonderful miracles we were enabled to secure what was then known as 'Stone's Folly,' a great mansion patterned after an English castle, one mile west of Washburn College in Topeka, Kansas."

How marvelously God made all things work together for good when we wholly committed our ways unto Him and left our case in His hands. Instead of taking up the work that we had, God had a greater, and grander work for us to do. If we had not fully obeyed the Scriptures to "resist not evil," and showed a Christian spirit, I am afraid we would not have received the baptism of the Holy Spirit. God had taught us that we were not only to preach the Word, but to practice it, and have it wrought out in our lives if we were to have His best.

This chapter is an edited version of what first appeared in **The Life of Charles F. Parham** *by his wife, Sarah E. Parham. The book was first published in 1930. It gives the best historical look into the Parham's life and early ministry in Topeka.*

Charles F. Parham
Sometimes the former Methodist minister preached in
clerical robes as shown in this photo.
Apostolic Faith Report
(Used by Permission)

$$Chapter\ 3$$

THE STORY OF THE ORIGIN OF THE ORIGINAL APOSTOLIC OR PENTECOSTAL MOVEMENTS

By Charles F. Parham

We opened the Bible school at Topeka, Kansas in October, 1900. To which we invited all ministers and Christians who were willing to forsake all, sell what they had, give it away, and enter the school for study and prayer, where all of us together might trust God for food, fuel, rent and clothing. The purpose of this school was to fit men and women to go to the ends of the earth to preach, "This Gospel of the Kingdom" as a witness to all the world before the end of the age (Matt. 24).

Our purpose in this Bible school was not to learn these things in our heads only but have each thing in the Scriptures wrought out in our hearts. And that every command that Jesus Christ gave should be literally obeyed.

No one paid board or tuition, the poor were fed, the sick were entertained and healed, and from day to day, week to week and month to month, with no sect or mission or known source of income back of us, God supplied our every need, and He was our all sufficiency in all things.

In December of 1900 we had had our examination upon the subject of repentance, conversion, consecration, sanctification, healing and the soon coming of the Lord. We had reached in our studies a problem. What about the 2nd Chapter of Acts? I had felt for years that any missionary going to the foreign field should preach in the language of the natives. That if God had ever equipped His ministers in that way He could do it today. That if Balaam's mule could stop in the middle of the road and give the first preacher that went out for money a "bawling out" in Arabic that anybody today ought to be able to preach in any language of the world if they had horse sense enough to let God use their tongue and throat. But still I believed our experience should tally exactly with the Bible. And neither sanctification nor the anointing that abideth taught by Stephen Merritt and others tallied with the 2nd chapter of Acts. Having heard so many different religious bodies claim different proofs as the evidence of their having the Pentecostal baptism, I set the students at work studying out diligently what was the Bible evidence of the baptism of the Holy Ghost, that we might go before the world with something, that was indisputable because it tallied absolutely with the Word.

Leaving the school for three days at this task, I went to Kansas City for three days services. I returned to the school on the morning preceding watch night services in the year 1900.

At about 10 o'clock in the morning I rang the bell calling all the students into the chapel to get their report on the matter in hand. To my astonishment they all had the same story, that while different things occurred when the Pentecostal blessing fell, that the indisputable proof on each occasion was, that they spake with other tongues. About 75 people beside the school which consisted of 40 students, had gathered for the watch night service. A mighty spiritual power filled the entire school.

Sister Agnes N. Ozman, (now LaBerge) asked that hands might be laid upon her to receive the Holy Spirit as she hoped to go to foreign fields. At first I refused not having the experience myself. When being further pressed to do it, humbly in the name of Jesus, I laid my hand upon her head and prayed. I had scarcely repeated three dozen sentences when a glory fell upon her, a halo seemed to surround her head and face, and she began speaking in the Chinese language, and was unable to speak English for three days. When she tried to write in English to tell us of her experience she wrote in the Chinese language, copies of which we still have in newspapers printed at that time.

Seeing this marvelous manifestation of the restoration of Pentecostal power, we removed the beds from a dormitory on the upper floor, and there for two nights and three days we continued as a school to wait upon God. We felt that God was no respecter of persons and what He had so graciously poured out upon one, He would upon all.

Those three days of tarrying were wonderful days of blessings. We all got past any begging or pleading, we knew the blessing was ours. With ever swelling tides of praise and thanksgiving and worship, interspersed with singing we waited for the coming of the Holy Spirit.

On the night of January 3rd, I preached at the Free Methodist Church in the City of Topeka telling them what had already happened, and that I expected upon returning the entire school to be baptized in the Holy Spirit. On returning to the school with one of the students, we ascended to the second flood, and passing down along the corridor in the upper room, heard most wonderful sounds. The door was slightly ajar, the room was lit with only coal oil lamps. As I pushed open the door I found the room was filled with a sheen of white light above the brightness of the lamps.

Twelve ministers of different denominations, who were in the school, were filled with the Holy Spirit and spoke with other tongues. Some were sitting, some still kneeling, others standing with hands upraised. There was no violent physical manifestation, though some trembled under the power of the glory that filled them.

Sister Stanley, an elderly lady, came across the room as I entered, telling me that just before I entered tongues of fire were sitting above their heads.

When I beheld the evidence of the restoration of Pentecostal power, my heart was melted in gratitude to God for what my eyes had seen. For years I had suffered terrible persecutions for preaching holiness and healing and the soon coming of the Lord. I fell to my knees behind a table unnoticed by those upon whom the power of Pentecost had fallen to pour out my heart to God in thanksgiving. All at once they began to sing, "Jesus Lover of my Soul" in at least six different languages, carrying the different parts but with a more angelic voice than I had ever listened to in all my life.

After praising God for some time, I asked Him for the same blessing. He distinctly made it clear to me that He raised me up and trained me to declare this mighty truth to the world, and if I was willing to stand for it, with all the persecutions, hardships, trials, slander, scandal that it would entail, He would give me the blessing. And I said "Lord I will, if you will just give me this blessing." Right then there came a slight twist in my throat, a glory fell over me and I began to worship God in the Swedish tongue, which later changed to other languages and continued so until the morning.

After preaching this for all these years with all the persecutions I have been permitted to go through with, misunderstanding and the treatment of false brethren, yet knowing all that, this blessing would bring to me, if I had the time and was back there again I'd take the same way.

No sooner was this miraculous restoration of Pentecostal power noised abroad, than we were besieged with reporters from Topeka papers, Kansas City, St. Louis and many other cities sent reporters who brought with them professors of languages, foreigners, government interpreters, and they gave the work the most crucial test.

One Government interpreter claimed to have heard twenty Chinese dialects distinctly spoken in one night. All agree that the students of the college were speaking in the languages of the world, and that with proper accent and intonation. There was no chattering, jabbering, or stuttering. Each one spoke clearly and distinctly in a foreign tongue, with earnestness, intensity and God given unction. The propriety and decency of the conduct of each member of the Bible school won the warmest comment from many visitors.

Our first public appearance after others had received the baptism of the Holy Spirit was in Kansas City, in the Academy of Music, about January 21st. The Kansas City papers loudly announced our coming. Two columns appeared in the **Kansas City Journal**, with large headlines on the front page. These headlines, being the largest on the front page, attracted the attention of the newsboys, and they not knowing a Pentecost from a holocaust ran wildly up and down the street crying their papers, "Pentecost, Pentecost, Pentecost, read all about the Pentecost."

I have on record the sermon preached on this occasion. The first upon the baptism of the Holy Ghost in all modern Pentecostal Apostolic Full Gospel movements. Also on file all that the papers had to say about these things in those days. Through great trials and persecutions we conducted the Bible school in the city of Topeka itself, then one in Kansas City.

*This article is also an excerpt from the book **The Life of Charles F. Parham: Founder of the Apostolic Faith Movement**. Although the book was written by Sarah Parham, Mr. Parham wrote this section. The first sermon preached after this mighty outpouring will follow in the next chapter. In this chapter, written after Parham's disappointing trip to the Azusa Street Mission in Los Angeles, the evangelist downplays any emotional manifestations that may have accompanied the Topeka blessing.*

Parham (on the left) and his band dressed in Bible land costumes.

Parham purchased the costumes from Tom Alley. He boasted they were the world's largest collecton of clothing from the Bible lands. Near the turn of the century, many attended Parham's meetings to view the colorful robes.

Apostolic Faith Report
(Used by Permission)

Chapter 4

BAPTIJM OF THE HOLY GHOJT.
THE JPEAKING IN OTHER TONGUEJ AND JEAL-
ING OF THE CHURCH AND BRIDE.

By Charles F. Parham

Since there are so many teachings today of self-ordained leaders of more or less human unction and truth, yet who fall into dreadful errors, it behooves us to "try the spirits," to prove all things by the Word of God. That error is the most dangerous which contains the most truth. Yea, error would fall of its own weight if not upheld by pillars of truth. We also find that wherever error exists it is marked by the intensity of propagation and seeming blindness of its disseminators to its utter unscripuralness.

The Word of God is perverted to suit their own convenience, until onward rushing through deserts barren or mountain wildernesses, they are lost to sight of sane and wiser men, wrecked on the crater of modern seething religious volcanic disturbances.

Many dear sheep of the tender Shepherd's fold, failing to find proper food either through the narrowness of self appointed leaders, or through failing to take the true teaching and light from men sent of God, have done what this little anecdote illustrates. Down in Texas there is difficulty in getting sheep over sloughs. A goat is sent ahead. The sheep nearly break their necks in following. So God's sheep are today led by goats into many arid pastures; starved, bleating flocks are eating the wool off each other, proselyting, denouncing all others who do not feed in the same pasture as themselves, while they feed upon the cacti and sage brush of wildest fanaticism, led by men whose so-called "divine revelations" are vain as mad-men's dreams, the unction of overwrought imaginations of self exaltation and esteem.

We have found the sweet relief of being shut away with the Word of God, where we may learn what He says and hear Him speak.

There are so many today claiming divine leadership, who say they are sealing the Bride, setting the true church in order by the baptism of water, etc. We feel led to declare the sealing of the Bride and setting the Body, the Church in order, is the work of the Godhead, not man's work.

Let us view the Scripture on this point. This very precious fact is noted, the sealed ones escape the plagues and wraths of the last days. Now is the seal of such a nature as to cause us to know when we are sealed, not to be deceived by the fallible sealings of men? Counterfeit sealings being abroad assures us it is time for the true sealing to take place. Wherever the counterfeit exists, the real must also. When we heard and studied the pretended claims of medical, mental, and Christian sciences, hypnotism, etc., we said, "God has the real of which these sorceries are the counterfeit." We found Him who bare our sicknesses (Matt. 8:17) and was lifted up for us even as Moses lifted up the serpent in the wilderness, (for healing) (John 3:14).

When beholding the power of spiritualism, for though 99 percent of it is slight of hand it does contain certain forces, as the possession of mediums, speaking under the control of evil spirits, etc. We said, God has the real of this; and, lo, when the power of Pentecost came we found the real, and everyone who has received the Baptism of the Holy Spirit has again spoken in tongues, having the same confounding evidence of Acts 2nd chapter, also 10:44-48 and 19:6.

Again, when like the witch of Endor, they materialize spirits, we said, God has the real, that He may be glorified and we find this in our coming redemption.

For years we have prayed for this present truth given in this book, simply that again we might throw down the rod of God's truth like Aaron of old--to utterly confound these workers of magic; leaders of anti-Christian seditious iniquity, the leaven of which worketh exceedingly now, preparing the way of the Anti-Christ.

Note where the 144,000 are sealed (Rev. 7). These are considered by nearly all students of the Scripture to refer to the Bride.*This sealing is not accomplished by man or water baptism, or the following of certain leaders, but is accomplished by the baptism of the Holy Ghost as recorded in Acts 2.

"Now He which established us with you in Christ and hath anointed us in God; who hath also sealed us and given us the earnest of the Spirit in our hearts" (2 Cor. 1:21-22).

"And grieve not the Holy Spirit of God whereby ye are sealed unto the day of redemption" (Eph. 4:30).

"After that ye believed, ye were sealed by the Holy Spirit of promise, which is the earnest of our inheritance" (Eph. 1:13-14). These verses clearly prove that it was the Holy Spirit promised.

"Behold, I send the promise of the Father upon you, but tarry ye in the city of Jerusalem until ye be endued with power from on high" (Luke 24:49).

---

*If this was the case when Parham was writing, it is not the case today. Ed.

This promise, when fulfilled was followed by such unmistakable evidence that no one can doubt it who has received it. Thousands of Christians profess this sealing as well as the baptism of the Holy Ghost, yet the Bible evidence is lacking in their lives. We want to say it is unscriptural to call mighty convictions, floods of joy, unctions or anointings, the baptism; there is but one. Jesus said, "John truly baptized with water; but ye shall be baptized with the Holy Ghost not many days hence" (Acts 1:5).

"But ye shall receive power after that the Holy Ghost has come upon you; and ye shall be witnesses unto me both in Jerusalem, and in all Judea, and in Samaria, and unto the uttermost part of the earth" (Acts 1:8).

Now all Christians credit the fact that we are to be the recipients of the Holy Spirit, but each have their private interpretations as to His visible manifestations; some claim shouting, leaping, jumping and falling in trances, while others put stress upon inspiration, unction and divine revelation. Probably the greatest mistake has been of thinking "the anointing that abideth" (I John 2:27), which the disciples received in the upper chamber when Christ breathed upon them, (John 20:22), the real baptism of the Holy Spirit. But by a careful study of Acts 1: 8, we find that the power was to make them witnesses. The modern idea of shouting, groaning and screaming, performed in imitation of supposed drunken disciples, is a misinterpretation of their actions; because the disciples by speaking various languages which were not understood by many in the audience (speaking as the Spirit gave them utterance) sounded like the mutterings of drunken men. These Galilean fishermen were not only witnessing to their own nation, but to the uttermost parts of the earth. The assembled Jews from different countries heard them speak the marvelous works of God in their own tongues wherein they were born.

This scene being true the same evidence would follow today as at that time, if we also are privileged to be recipients of the baptism of the Holy Ghost; proving they did receive this promised power, for which they tarried. How much more reasonable it would be for modern Holy Ghost teachers to first receive a BIBLE EVIDENCE, such as the disciples, instead of trying to get the world to take their word for it. And how much better it would be for our modern missionaries to obey the injunction of Jesus to tarry for the same power: instead of wasting thousands of dollars, and often their lives in the vain attempt to become conversant in almost impossible tongues which the Holy Ghost could so freely speak. Knowing all languages, He could as easily speak through us one, as another were our tongues and vocal chords fully surrendered to His domination and in connection realize the precious assurance of the sealing of the Holy Ghost, knowing it by the same evidence as received by the one hundred and twenty on the day of Pentecost, of Cornelius and his household, and of the church at Ephesus.*

MODERN RECEPTION OF THE HOLY GHOST

Since the days of the Apostolic church a few authentic cases of the baptism of the Holy Spirit are recorded.

We have found that the early Catholic Fathers upon reaching the coast of Japan spoke in the native tongue; that the Irvingites, a sect that arose under the teachings of Irving, a Scotsman, during the last century, received not only the eight recorded gifts of I Cor. 12, but also the speaking in other tongues, which the Holy Ghost reserved as the evidence of His oncoming. A gentleman and his wife, whose names we have forgotten, received their Pentecost and

---

*In the earliest days of the Pentecostal outpouring, it was common to believe that missionaries would go foreign countries and be able to minister without learning the language of the land. Parham and others believed that the gift of tongues would be sufficient. Unfortunately, many sincere missionaries were disappointed and left their field of labor without the success for which they had hoped. Ed.

spoke in the Italian language. Jenny Glassey of St. Louis, after a special time of tarrying received her Pentecost and was enabled to speak, sing, write and interpret certain African dialects. After being a missionary in Africa she became a resident of Jerusalem.

A very pious man, member of the Baptist Church, Marshaltown, Iowa, received the baptism of the Holy Spirit. His church not honoring the presence and power of the Holy Ghost in their midst, he was gathered in by the Spiritualists who persuaded him that his Pentecostal power was but a manifestation of their nefarious mediumship. Losing his salvation and spiritual power, he became sick and afflicted, lost his mind and is today a complete wreck. How many like cases there are in this world we know not, but we do know that the narrowness of modern church Christianity, by refusing to believe and receive true Bible doctrines has driven many thousands unto Spiritualism, Theosophy, Christian Science and infidelity.

Thousands have received what they termed and supposed was the baptism of the Holy Spirit, but which was in reality the anointing that abideth. The first teaching on this subject that we became conversant with was that the witness of our sanctification was the baptism of the Holy Spirit. The fallacy of this is easily proven. For by one offering He has perfected forever them that are sanctified. Whereof the Holy Ghost also is a witness unto us (Heb. 10: 14-15).

The word "also" in the 15th verse precludes the teaching that the witness to our sanctification is the baptism of the Holy Spirit, for it proves that the witness to our sanctification is given by the Holy Spirit the same as our justification, and if we should claim the one at sanctification to be the baptism of the Holy Spirit, the word "also" would force us to claim the witness of justification to be the baptism of the Holy Spirit.

The fact is in justification and sanctification, the Holy Spirit witnesses to our hearts of the inwrought work of the atonement, His personal work as the third person in the

Trinity which is a gift not a grace, is not obtained in justification or sanctification.

Later came a wave of teaching that the Holy Spirit was really a gift not received at the time of sanctification. Accordingly hundreds sought for the Spirit in this way, receiving a special anointing such as the disciples received in the upper chamber, when Jesus breathed upon them saying, "Receive ye the Holy Ghost" (John 20:22). Therefore having the anointing that abideth and teacheth like the disciples upon whom Jesus breathed, their eyes were opened, the teaching of the Scriptures became clear and precious, the reception of the Holy Ghost as their Anointer and Teacher (Luke 24:45). The disciples obtained all that modern Holy Ghost people have, and yet this occurrence was ten days before Pentecost. Hungering and thirsting for the realization of the same mighty power in God's people today, which is theirs by divine light (for we truly are in the days of the restitution of all things which God has spoken by the mouth of all His holy prophets since the world began (Acts 3:21), we made a study of all teachings upon this subject and found none had really the experience of Acts chapter 2.

Pursuing our studies, we visited institutions of deep religious thought, which were reported as having the power of the Holy Ghost; yet these all failed to tally with the account in Acts. After careful study, we returned from an extended trip through the east and Canada with profound conviction that no one in these days was really enjoying the power of a personal Pentecost, while many were anointed above measure. We ourselves had known the power of the Holy Ghost in our lives to a wonderful degree for many years, and had such wonderful anointings that we were carried far beyond ourselves, many times for ten, fifteen and twenty minutes words of living truth (our minds took no part, but in which we became an interested listener) flowed from our lips; yet this was but the anointing that abideth, not the baptism of the Holy Ghost as many declared it to be. This anointing is sufficient under all circumstances for needed inspiration when speaking in our tongue, but if you desire a personal baptism of the Holy Ghost, the sealing power, escaping plagues, and putting you in the position to become a part of the Body, the Bride or the Man-Child, seek the Holy Ghost.

It was prophesied, "With men of other tongues and other lips will I speak unto this people, and yet for all that will they not hear me, saith the Lord" (I Cor. 14:21).

Many say to us, if we were going to a foreign land we should need to speak in other tongues, what need have we of it among our own people? According to the above prophecy, God intends to use the speaking in other tongues in preaching to our people. For centuries men have been sent preaching in their own tongues to their own nation, until the people have come to believe that they are simply propagating some self-constructed creed or ideas for their pecuniary benefit.

In the close of the age, God proposes to send forth men and women preaching in languages they know not a word of, which when interpreted the hearers will know is truly a message from God, spoken through lips of clay by the power of the Holy Ghost. This is truly the acme of inspiration, prayed for every Sabbath and desired by all true ministers of God.

Do you mean to say that John Wesley and others since, did not have this baptism? Exactly; he and many since have enjoyed a mighty anointing that abideth, and spoke like the holy men of old as they were moved by the Holy Ghost but the power of this Pentecostal baptism of the Holy Spirit is a different thing entirely.

The baptism of the Holy Spirit is especially given now as the sealing. Therefore the sureness of the last days.

On Oct. 15, 1900, we were led to open in Topeka, Kansas, a Bible school which became widely known sometime later as "the College of Bethel." Its unique features and teachings became subjects of the daily papers throughout the land. Its only textbook was the Bible; its only object utter abandonment in obedience to the commandments of Jesus, however unconventional and impractical this might seem to the world today. About forty students entered. No collections were taken, no solicitations, no board, no tuition charged. No difference was made whether the students had any means to offer or whether they did not; but one thing was strictly required that they should obey and seek to live the commandments of Jesus. Under these circumstances, day after day, week after week, and month after month, God was faithful in supplying all our needs, yea, "no good things did He withhold from them who walked uprightly." With a people thus given up to God, who more fully obeyed the commands of Jesus, and in a stricter sense had "all things in common" than any other Bible school in the world, we were enabled to sink deeper into the things of God, and to obtain a more comprehensive view of the heights and depths, lengths and breadths of God's eternal purpose, which He purposed through Jesus Christ our Lord.

Thus in obedience to John 14: 15-17, proved our love by keeping His commandments, therefore had a more perfect right to obtain the Comforter than many of God's servants today, who are nearly given up, but not entirely to obey all His commandments.

When we speak thus many say to us, "Oh, but we do obey all the commands of Jesus." To which we reply, "Do you give to every man that asketh of you? Do you really take no thought of what ye shall eat or drink, where with all ye shall be clothed, or of the morrow? Do you go into all the world and preach the Gospel to every creature? Do you obey the command to go, teach, preach, and heal? Have you heard that Jesus said, except a man forsake all, he cannot be my disciple: and whosoever will forsake houses and lands, and father and mother and all for my sake, shall have a hundred fold in this world, and in the world to come life everlasting?"

This is enough, for long 'ere we reach the hundred-fold, the forsaking all part, they hold up their hands in utter rebellion, saying, "Oh, the Lord did not mean just what He said, many of those things were only meant for the apostles and only to be spiritually interpreted to us." So they sit in peace when there is work to be done, or be carried through on flowery beds of ease to their eternal disease.

Nearly all of the students had been religious workers of considerable spiritual growth and attainment. Like many of our readers, said they had received the baptism of the Holy Ghost a number of years ago, but in spite of this we continued to teach what we believed to be in the Word of God, and in the mind of Jesus; a mighty baptism such as the disciples received of old, to make His saints today worldwide powers for good, to the end that this gospel might be preached to all the world as a witness, "To remove the covering cast over all the face of the earth, for we believe this to be the will of God, and the accomplishment of the same well pleasing in His sight."

In the closing days of the fall term of 1900, we had our examination on repentance, justification, consecration, sanctification, and healing. As there yet remained a few days before the opening of the new year, the students were required to carefully study the subject of the baptism of the Holy Spirit. The main object of this study was to discover the real Bible evidence of this baptism so that we might know and obtain it, instead of being confused by the chaotic claims of modern Holy Ghost teachers.

On New Year's night, Miss Agnes N. Ozman of Beatrice, Nebraska, a missionary lady who had attended several Bible schools and done considerable religious work; one who had had mighty anointings and had for years the "anointing that abideth" which she mistook for the baptism was convinced of her need of a personal Pentecost. She desired hands laid upon her that she might receive the gift of the Holy Ghost. During invocation of hands prayer was offered, she was filled with the Holy Ghost and spake with other tongues as the Spirit gave utterance. Upon beholding this marvelous restoration of apostolic power in our midst, all became hungry, earnestly desiring a personal realization of the same in our lives; remembering that Peter had said, "This promise is to you and to your children, and to all that are afar off, even as many as the Lord our God shall call" (Acts 2:39).

Scarcely eating or sleeping, the school with one accord waited upon God. On the night of the 3rd of January, 1901, we were all assembled in an upper room. A most wonderful power pervaded the atmosphere, and twelve students were filled with the Holy Ghost and began to speak with other tongues as the Spirit gave them utterance; while several in the room saw above their heads, cloven tongues of fire, as in the days of old. Thus was the church militant again permitted to realize the baptism of the Holy Spirit, which has since then been given to not only others in the school but to those in other cities and states.

Like seekers for justification, sanctification and healing some then and others since, have sought for and failing to obtain the baptism, turned back, saying it was either not for them or deriding it as mere bramble which had no special import or value. The fact remains that it is the baptism of the Holy Spirit of promise, that seals the Bride and the same baptism that puts us in one Body (the church).

We wish here to give a little advice, no one in the school or in our work or meetings since, who protested that they had received the baptism of the Holy Spirit, have ever obtained it; while those who have freely acknowledged and given glory to God for all His wonderful anointings, manifestations and gifts of the Spirit, humbly surrendering the claim to this baptism, have obtained the power desired, and gone forth speaking in tongues as the authoritative evidence.

Many in our meetings have said, "Oh, I have had the baptism of the Holy Spirit for years." And, many with an extra boast of human unction, "I have received the baptism of fire."

We have heard of a Bible school that made most marvelous claims in regard to the baptism of the Holy Spirit.

Like many individuals above spoken of in different meetings, said, "We have received the baptism of the Holy Spirit, but as we are bent upon the world's evangelization, we must have this." This Bible school sought in vain, month after month for the speaking in other languages.

Now we want to say to private individuals or to schools, that the speaking in other tongues is an inseparable part of the baptism of the Holy Spirit distinguishing it from all previous works; and that no one has received baptism of the Holy Spirit who has not a Bible evidence to show for it. As pardon is received as a result of sincere repentance, restitution and surrender; sanctification received as the result of entire consecration; so the speaking in other tongues is received as the result of this baptism. The Holy Spirit, thru witnessing to the work of Calvary wrought in our lives, in justification and sanctification, reserves the speaking in other tongues as the evidence of His own incoming. Many say, "Oh, I have the gift of healing or discernment or some other gift that is as good to me as the speaking in other tongues as an evidence that I have the Holy Spirit." Yet in spite of the rebellious toss of the head and seeming disregard for the Word of God, the fact is the gifts of wisdom, knowledge, faith, healing, working of miracles, prophecy, discernment of spirits, and interpretation of tongues were fully manifested in Old Testament prophets, and New Testament disciples before the day of Pentecost; and many have received inspiration, teaching and anointing, for holy men of old spake as they were moved by the Holy Ghost (II Peter 1:21); yet, His personal baptism was not yet ministered.

The Bible records this fact and it seems strange to us that people would dare dispute or try to compass it; that on the day of Pentecost (Acts 2) the manifest evidence resulting from this baptism, which confounded and astounded the multitudes was, that seventeen different nationalities heard them speak in their own tongue wherein they were born. To this was added the testimony of Peter (16 verse),

"This is that which was spoken by Joel, the prophet." And again, "Therefore being by the right hand of God exalted, and having received of the Father the promise of the Holy Ghost, He hath shed forth this, which you now see and hear" (33 verse). "For the promise is unto you, and to your children, and to all that are afar off, even as many as the Lord our God shall call" (39 verse).

Now if this were the only time that speaking with other tongues was the evidence of the Holy Spirit, it would be sufficient; but it is found repeatedly, yea every time the Holy Ghost fell and the evidence was noted, it proved to be this same one of speaking with tongues.

When Peter had been convinced by a series of visions that the Gentiles were to become the recipients of full salvation, being called to preach at the house of Cornelius, was accompanied by Christian Jews from Joppa, who though they had been followers of the meek and lowly Nazarene, they still considered that salvation was of the Jews.

"While Peter yet spake these words, the Holy Ghost fell on all of them which heard the Word" (Acts 10:44).

"And they of the circumcision which believed were astonished, as many as came with Peter, because that on the Gentiles also was poured out the gift of the Holy Ghost. For they heard them speak with tongues, and magnify God" (Acts 10:46).

No doubt, they had contended with Peter on their journey thither regarding his new departure, whether the Gentiles were eligible to deeper spiritual attainments. It did not require a testimony from Cornelius, interspersed with leaping or shouting or any of the other modern manifestations of the so-called Holy Ghost power, to prove to these circumcised Jews that Cornelius had the gift of the Holy Ghost, when they heard him and his company speak with tongues. This scene no doubt had become familiar to them since the day of Pentecost, not only hearing of it from Jerusalem, but most certainly have witnessed the same scene in Joppa and elsewhere. When they heard them speak with tongues, they were convinced that the Gentiles also were brought nigh by the blood of Jesus; and become privileged with the endowment of power. At this climax, Peter, seeing that the manifestation of the Spirit's presence had utterly refuted every argument of the brethren, said in triumph, "Can any man forbid water, that these should be baptized, which have received the Holy Spirit as well as we?" (Acts 10:47).

"As well as we," signifies that the brethren who came with Peter from Joppa, had received the Holy Spirit the same as Peter did on the day of Pentecost. In relating his experience at Jerusalem, Peter speaks thus, "And as I began to speak, the Holy Ghost fell on them, as on us at the beginning. Then remembered I the word of the Lord, how that He said, "John indeed baptized with water, but ye shall be baptized with the Holy Ghost. For as much then as God gave them the like gift as He did unto us, who was I, that I could withstand God?" (Acts 11:15-17).

Nor is this all the proof that speaking with other tongues is the evidence of the Holy Spirit. Yea, all Scripture upon this subject agree; only modern teachers disagree.

When Paul went down to Ephesus, he said unto them, "Have ye received the Holy Spirit since ye believed? They said unto him, we have not so much as heard whether there be any Holy Ghost" (Acts 19:2) ["whether the Holy Ghost be yet given" (revised version)].

After finding out that they had simply been baptized under John's baptism unto repentance, he taught them the way more perfectly, baptizing them in the name of the Lord Jesus.

"And when Paul laid his hands upon them, the Holy Ghost came on them and they spake with tongues, and prophesied" (Acts 19:6). To prophesy, in the Old Testament sense, was to foretell events; but Paul says, "But he that prophesieth speaketh unto men to edification, and exhortation and comfort" (Cor. 14:3). While John the Revelator, says, "The testimony of Jesus is the spirit of prophecy" (Rev. 19:10).

In later years when speaking in tongues was a common feature of the worship of the Corinthian church, they wrote Paul for instruction as to how to conduct themselves, as the individuals did not understand the languages spoken--there not always being interpreters present--it brought more or less confusion.

Paul answering declares, "I would that ye all spake with tongues" (I Cor. 14:5) and, "I thank my God, I speak with tongues more than ye all" (verse 18). Thus, showing that he also had the same evidence that we so many times noted. And again, he said, "Forbid not to speak with tongues" (39 verse).

We are often asked, why is it that so many leaders of so-called Apostolic churches have many, or nearly all of the signs that were to follow believers, recorded in Mark 16:17, 18, except the speaking with new tongues? We always answer, "Modern leaders and Holy Ghost teachers all have their private evidence of their so-called gift of the Holy Ghost; while they have failed to seek, obtain and honor the only Bible sign given as the evidence of the baptism of the Holy Ghost."

This sermon was preached at the Academy of Music in Kansas City, Missouri only twenty-one days after the Topeka Outpouring. It was Parham's first sermon on Pentecost and was originally published in 1901 in **Kol Kare Bomidbar: A Voice Crying in the Wilderness**. *The sermon was edited for spelling and punctuation.*

Lilian Thistlethwaite
Apostolic Faith Report
(Used by Permission)

Chapter 5

THE WONDERFUL HISTORY OF THE LATTER RAIN

By Lilian Thistlethwaite

The First Shower of the Latter Rain--Bethel Bible School

In the year 1900, Charles F. Parham, and his wife and family and a number of Bible students, gathered in the Bethel Bible School to study the Word of God, using no text book excepting, the Bible.

The building procured for this school was known by the people of Topeka, Kansas, as the "Stone Mansion" or "Stone's Folly" because it had been patterned after an English castle, and he, having failed to "count the cost," was unable to finish in the style planned. The beautiful carved staircase and finished woodwork of cedar of Lebanon, spotted pine, cherry wood and bird's eye maple, ended on the third floor with plain wood and common paint.

The outside was finished in red brick and white stone with winding stairs that went up to an observatory on the front of the highest part of the building. There was also a cupola at the back of the building and two domes built on either side. Into one of these a door was cut, making a room large enough for a small stove, a table and a chair. This was known as the "Prayer Tower." Volunteers from among the students took their turn of three hours watch; so day and night prayer ascended unto God. Sometimes a student would desire to spend the night in waiting before the Lord and this privilege was allowed.

When the building was dedicated for the school, while in prayer, on the top of the building, Captain Tuttle, a godly man, who was with Mr. Parham said he saw (in a vision) just above the building a "vast lake of fresh water about to overflow, containing enough to satisfy every thirsty soul." This we believe was the promise of the Pentecostal baptism which followed later.

There were about forty persons gathered here including the children. The method of study was to take a subject, learn the references on that subject, also where each quotation was found, and present to the class in recitation as though they were seekers, praying for the anointing of the Holy Spirit to be upon the message in such a way as to bring conviction.

Mr. Parham also taught through lectures. I will never forget the one he gave on the Song of Solomon. How we were all lifted into the heavenlies and the room seemed filled with the glory of God's presence!

It was just before the Christmas holidays that we took up the study of the Holy Ghost. Mr. Parham was going to Kansas City to conduct meetings there and to bring some friends back with him to spend Christmas and be present for the watch night meeting. Before leaving the following is the substance of what he said, "Students, as I have studied the teachings in the various Bible schools and full gospel movements, conviction, conversion, healing and sanctification are taught virtually the same, but on the baptism there is a difference among them. Some accept Steven

Merrit's teaching of baptism at sanctification, while others say this is only the anointing and there is a baptism received through the 'laying on of hands' or the gift of the Holy Ghost, yet they agree on no definite evidence. Some claim this fulfillment of promise 'by faith' without any special witness while others, because of wonderful blessings or demonstrations, such as shouting or jumping. Though I honor the Holy Ghost in anointing power both in conversion and in sanctification, yet I believe there is a greater revelation of His power. The gifts are in the Holy Spirit and with the baptism of the Holy Spirit the gifts, as well as the graces, should be manifested. Now, students, while I am gone see if there is not some evidence given of the baptism so there may be no doubt on the subject.

"We see the signs already being fulfilled that mark the soon coming of the Lord and I believe with John Wesley that at Christ's second coming the church will be found with the same power that the apostles and the early church possessed."

Thus closed the regular Bible lessons, for a time, but there was individual and collective prayer and study of the Bible continuously.

On Mr. Parham's return to the school with his friends, he asked the students whether, they had found any Bible evidence of the baptism of the Holy Spirit. The answer was, unanimous, "speaking in other tongues."

Services were held daily and each night. There was a hallowed hush over the entire building. All felt the influence of a mighty presence in our midst. Without any special direction, all moved in harmony. I remember Mrs. Parham saying, "Such a spirit of unity prevails that even the children are at peace, while the very air is filled with expectancy. Truly He is with us, and had something more wonderful for us than we have known before."

The service on New Year's night was especially spiritual and each heart was filled with the hunger for the will of God to be done in them. One of the students, a lady who had been in several other Bible schools, asked Mr. Parham, to lay hands upon her that she might receive the Holy Spirit. As he prayed, her face lighted up with the glory of God and she began to speak with "other tongues." She afterward told us she had received a few words while in the prayer tower, but now her English was taken from her and with floods of joy and laughter she praised God in other languages.

There was very little sleeping among any of us that night. The next day still being unable to speak English, she wrote on a piece of paper, "Pray that I may interpret."

The following day was Thursday. This day, Mr. Parham observed as a day of special prayer and waiting upon the Lord. From 9 A. M. to 3 P. M., he believes to be the six hours Christ spent on the cross, so these hours were observed in special waiting on the Lord that all that was purchased upon Calvary should be wrought out in our individual lives. The "broken body" or the atonement for healing was especially honored in these meetings.

On this particular day, the baptism of the Holy Ghost was sought earnestly, but no one received the gift. Having other duties in the home I had not searched the Scriptures to know the Bible evidence, nor heard the decision of those who had, but in my own mind concluded as the gifts are in the Holy Ghost any of the nine gifts would prove the baptism; and as Paul said, "desire earnestly the best gifts." I felt "faith" was the most to be desired and was looking for this gift in some way to be manifested.

An upper room was set apart for tarrying before the Lord, and here we spent every spare moment in audible or silent prayer, in song or in just waiting upon Him. There was no confusion, as only one prayed audibly at a time, and when more than one sang it was the same hymn. It was truly a time of precious waiting. His presence was very real and the heart-searchings definite.

Mr. Parham was holding night services in Topeka and before leaving he said, "I don't suppose I shall be able to understand any of you when I return."

Still I was not looking for "tongues," but some evidence from God (I didn't know of what nature) that would convince me I had the baptism. We prayed for ourselves, we prayed for one another. I never felt so little and utterly nothing before. A scrap of paper charred by a fire is the best description I can give of my feelings. Then through the Spirit this message came to my soul, "Praise Him for the baptism for He does come in by faith through the laying on of hands." Then a great joy came into my soul and I began to say, "I praise Thee." My tongue began to get thick and great floods of laughter came into my heart. I could no longer think words of praise, for my mind was sealed, but my mouth was filled with a rush of words I didn't understand. I tried not to laugh for I feared to grieve the Spirit. I tried to praise Him in English but could not, so I just let the praise come as it would in the new language given, with floodgates of glory wide open. He had come to me, even to me to speak not of Himself but to magnify the Christ, and oh, what a wonderful, wonderful Christ was revealed. Then I realized I was not alone for all around me I heard great rejoicing while others spoke in tongues and magnified God. I think Mrs. Parham's language was the most perfect. Immediately following came the interpretation, a beautiful poem of praise and worship to Christ, proving the words of the Savior, "When the Comforter is come . . . he shall testify of me . . . shall not speak of himself . . . shall teach you all things and bring to your remembrance whatsoever I have said unto you."

Then, as with a simultaneous move we began to sing together each one singing in his own new language in perfect harmony. As we sang, "All Hail the Power of Jesus' Name," and other familiar tunes, it would be impossible to describe the hallowed glory of His presence in our midst.

The cloven tongues of fire had been seen by some when the evidence had been received. Mr. Parham came into the room while we were standing singing. Kneeling, he thanked God for the scene he was allowed to witness, then asking God if it was His will that he should stand for the baptism of the Holy Spirit as he had for healing, to give him the Bible evidence. His prayer, was answered, the gift bestowed, and the persecution came also.

Never had such a hallowed joy, such a refined glory or, such an abundance of peace, ever come into my life. The Comforter had come and the words of Jesus being brought continually to my remembrance, as Scripture after Scripture was unfolded by day and by night. I was filled with a settled rest and quietness my soul had never known before. I lived in the heavenlies.

As we went into meetings it seemed impossible that any could resist the messages given. Some understanding the languages were convinced but others fulfilled the prophecy, "With men of other tongues and other lips will I speak unto this people; and yet for, all that they will not hear me, saith the Lord" (I Cor. 14:21). On one occasion a Hebrew Rabbi was present as one of the students, a young married man, read the lesson from the Bible. After services he asked for the Bible from which the lesson was read. The Bible was handed him, and he said, "No not that one, I want to see the Hebrew Bible. That man read in the Hebrew tongue."

At another time while Mr. Parham was preaching he used another language for some time during the sermon. At the close a man arose and said, " I am healed of my infidelity; I have heard in my own tongue the 23rd Psalm that I learned at my mother's knee. "

The Bible school building was sold. We moved to a building in Topeka where we stayed for a short time, then went to Kansas City. While living in Kansas City we heard that the building where Pentecost first fell was burned. This was not a surprise to us, as it had been turned into a road house and the rooms that once had heard only the voice of supplication and praise to God, had been desecrated by worldly revelry. Warning was given that such actions would not go unpunished, for the house was dedicated to the Lord from its highest place of observation to the cellar.

In Kansas City, Missouri, Mr. Parham held a Bible School, also meetings. During this time souls were saved, some received their baptism and others were healed. The persecutions were great and we were learning many lessons.

In the third year of the work God mightily vindicated the cause and many souls were saved, wonderful healings took place, and the falling of the Pentecostal baptism was very convincing.

I do not know to what denomination all belonged who received the baptism at Bethel Bible School, but some were Methodists, others Friends, and some Holiness, while many belonged to no denomination.

There were only white persons present at the first Pentecostal shower. No colored people were ever in the school. *

As Mrs. Parham's sister, it has been my privilege to be in their home or in touch with their, work continually. To witness Mr. Parham's zeal and untiring energy you would not believe it possible he had been a sufferer for years until healed by the power of God. The work of his ministry was conducted entirely on faith lines. He looked to the Lord to open the field of labor and was obedient to that which he felt to be His will, then left the results with God, who hath said, "His Word shall not return unto Him void." His family was dear to him. He enjoyed doing the little things about the home, caring for the children and giving the love service, which makes life worth living. Soon after they were married he was given some land in the country, and I remember him saying to my sister, "If the Lord would only let me, we would have a little home and raise chickens." But choosing the "better part," together they continued the life of service for others.

---

*This language, although considered appropriate when this was written, may be offensive today. It has been printed only to convey the author's original message, not to offend contemporary readers.

64

He taught as the discipline of the movement he represented and for his own life and practice, the keeping of the commandments of Jesus. He rejoiced in the opportunity to "overcome evil with good." He also practiced the command to "Give to every man that asketh of thee, and to him that would borrow of thee, turn not away," and God rewarded an hundred fold. Many times he gave the last cent he had, or clothes and food that would be needed the following day; but the Scripture obeyed brought the fulfillment of the promised "good measure" returned, even to the running over. A marked characteristic of his work was his ability to reach all classes, the rich and the cultured, the poor and the outcast of society, with the same touch of understanding that makes of one common brotherhood all God's creatures.

Having known the power of healing in his own life, and believing God's promises are the same today for those who could believe, he prayed for the sick who were healed, even as sinners were delivered from the power of sin through faith in the atonement. When Mrs. Parham first wrote me about the wonderful healings they were having among the people, I could hardly believe it possible. I knew Christ and the disciples healed the people and I also believed that Mr. Parham was healed, but I thought these were special cases. I had a physical disorder that had troubled me for years, I would try the Lord and see if He would heal now as when here in person. God, searching the heart, knoweth all things. How great His patience and tender mercies toward us! He graciously healed me.

Later, I contracted a cold resulting in a cough which instead of getting better grew worse until I was confined to bed. My mother and the others were anxious about me, feeling I should have a doctor. To this I could not consent for I had not only been healed myself but had seen many others healed through prayer. I remembered I had come for healing to prove God's promises, now I felt God was proving me. They were praying for me at Bethel Bible School where Mr. and Mrs. Parham were in charge, yet I still remained sick. Later, Mr. Parham came into my mother's home and prayed for me. I felt the healing virtue go through my body and was entirely delivered. I thank God for His great love for His children; that He has purchased not only salvation for the soul but also healing for the body, which is the temple of the Holy Ghost. I also thank God for His faithful messenger, who has been an inspiration and blessing to so many and truly given his life as a living sacrifice in service for others, though his faith was often tried, as by fire.

*This story was originally published in 1941 as part of a collection of sermons titled, **Selected Sermons of the Late Charles F. Parham and Sarah E. Parham**. Slight changes were made in spelling and punctuation.*

The Charles F. Parham Family
Top Row: Charles and Lilian Thistlethwaite
Middle Row: Esther, Sarah and Baby Wilford
Bottom Row: Claude and Phillip
Apostolic Faith Report
(Used by Permission)

Charles F. Parham's
band of Apostolic
workers.
(Parham is in the center)
Perhaps this is the
group from
Bethel Bible College.
Apostolic Faith Report
(Used by Permission)

Charles F. Parham

Agnes N. Ozman
Both sketches from the Kansas City Times
January 27, 1901
(Public Domain)

Chapter 6

WHERE THE LATTER RAIN FIRST FELL
THE FIRST ONE TO SPEAK IN TONGUES

By Agnes N. Ozman

In the fall of 1900 I went to a Bible school in Topeka, Kansas. We studied the Word and had much prayer,
not only in the school and in our rooms, but also in the
prayer tower, where a constant vigil of prayer was kept up
day and night.

At this school I had many feasts with the Master,
while I sought to make a full surrender to God. Much time
was given to meditating upon His Word and in praying for
the whole world.

A mission was conducted in the downtown district,
cottage meetings were held, and house to house visitation
carried on. The school was conducted on faith lines for we
trusted the Lord to supply all our needs, which He bounti-
fully did.

We were urged to seek for and to receive the promised baptism in the Holy Spirit. Our hearts became very

hungry for his enduement. We prayed earnestly and also fasted, as the Lord laid it upon us. During the last days of 1900 we had a special season of waiting before God, and He gave us blessed times of refreshing. Indeed, about three weeks before this, while three of us girls were in prayer, I spoke three words in another tongue. While I did not understand this manifestation then as I do now, yet it was a very precious and sacred experience, and was treasured in our hearts. Not feeling satisfied with the above experience and having a great burden within which I knew God could relieve. I decided, January 1,1901, to obey the Word and have hands laid upon me and prayer offered that I might receive the baptism in the Spirit. As this was done, I began to speak in an unknown tongue. Afterwards I saw my experience was somewhat similar to that in Ephesus (Acts 19:6).

After this I attended the mission with others and offered prayer, beginning in English, and then the Lord spoke through me, finishing the prayer in another tongue. One man who heard understood the language. It was very blessed to know that it was intelligible. This manifestation attracted much attention for it was new, and I was the first one to speak in tongues in these last days. How I long for the people to behold Christ, and that through me, God might glorify Himself!

We searched the Word for light on the subject of speaking in tongues. I was surprised to find so much in the New Testament on that subject. When heaven's glory filled my soul, so that I spoke in tongues, I urged upon others not to seek for tongues but for the baptism in the Holy Spirit. On January 3rd some thirteen others spoke in tongues during a time of waiting upon God. Other gifts were also manifested. "All these worketh the one and the same spirit, dividing to each one severally, even as he will" (I Cor. 12:11).

Our school home was carried on by each one doing a portion of the work, and sometimes friction and disobedience was manifested, but during this visitation from heaven there were blessed unity and love. The glory of God was wonderful! Praise be to God the glory abides to this day.

A continual feast is in my soul as I feed on the Word and pour out my soul in prayer, both in the known and in the unknown tongue for the lost. As I speak in tongues, my soul is blessed and lifted up as in I Cor. 14:4, and I wish that all might so speak. My heart is burdened for the church and I would that more were prophesying or preaching. Since "there are diversities of workings but the same God" we do need to urge upon His children to be surrendered to Him so He may have more channels through whom to work. "We are witnesses of these things; and so is the Holy Spirit whom God hath given to them that obey Him" (Acts 3:32).

Some time ago I tried but failed to have an article printed which I wrote calling attention to what I am sure God showed me was error. The article maintained that tongues was not the only evidence of the Spirit's baptism. When that article was refused I was much tempted by Satan, but God again graciously showed me He had revealed it to me, and satisfied my heart in praying that He might reveal this truth to others who would spread it abroad.

For awhile after the baptism I got into spiritual darkness, because I did as I see so many others are doing in these days, rested and revealed tongues and other demonstrations instead of resting alone in God.

My power to speak in tongues has not been lessened by giving up the errors which have become attached to this work, but instead it has increased. For all His blessings I praise Him. I am looking for the blessed hope and appearing of the glory of the great God and our Savior Jesus Christ.

December 30, 1908
Gospel Tabernacle
200 North 12th Street
Lincoln, Nebraska

*Miss Ozman's article was published in **The Latter Rain Evangel** in January 1909. The next chapter contains a longer article dealing with Miss Ozman's life and testimony.*

Chapter 7

WHAT GOD HATH WROUGHT IN THE LIFE OF AGNES N. OZMAN LABERGE

By Agnes N. Ozman Laberge

There were six of us children, Elizabeth, Etta, Edmund, Grant, Mary Ella, Roscoe C., Alfred Blaine and myself, Agnes Nevada. Our father's name was William L. Ozman and our mother's, Mary Ann Phillips.

I was born in Albany, Green County, Wisconsin on September 15th, 1870, on my father's thirty-third birthday. In the spring when still in long dresses we went in a covered wagon overland to Nebraska. We arrived in Lincoln, Nebraska on the 4th of July, 1871 and went south and a little west for about 24 miles. My father took a homestead in Highland, Gage County, Nebraska, where we lived until after I was 15 years old, and then we moved on another farm two miles west of Cortland, Nebraska. We lived there until after my mother's death.

How much sacrifice people do make to obtain an earthly home and how much more by the grace and power of God upon us and with the burden for souls the follow-ers of Jesus go through for Him. My parents endured great trials. They lived in a dugout, and I well remember when my father drove an ox team. We lived in serious poverty.

We all went to church and Sunday school at the Star school house some 22 miles away. Mother had us all stay in the church during preaching. My brother Roscoe, felt mother was hard on the boys for not letting them go up, as some other boys did, to play when meetings were held.

But later in life, they said mother was right. She also taught them never to play keeps when playing marbles, and my brother said he never did play keeps.* In later years, he said honesty was planted in his heart through mother's teaching and training.

My father sent us older children to school at Beatrice, Nebraska. I sat behind a colored girl one term and she said she became a Christian because I was good to her.** I heard of a colored women who could not read, and of a blind man, and oh, how happy I was to read the Bible to them, and to do this for Jesus. It will make every boy and girl very happy to do good to others.

We each worked at home and enjoyed helping with the duties about the home. Our parents read the Bible to us and taught us to pray. From my earliest remembrance I loved to hear about the Lord and wanted to follow Jesus. At family prayer I learned to bring my sins to Jesus and to know He forgave me. I do not remember when I was first

---

*This was a game of marbles where the winner kept the opponents marbles. It was considered by some to be a form of gambling.

**This language, although considered appropriate when this was written, may be offensive today. It has been printed only to convey the author's original message, not to offend contemporary readers.

forgiven of my sins. I thank God for the call of God to the children's hearts. The Bible says, "For whosoever shall call upon the name of the Lord shall be saved."

SCHOOL LIFE

For a time my father rented rooms in the city and my sister Elizabeth and I did light housekeeping when going to school. Often, it being so far home, we were in the city over Sunday. We attended the Methodist church in a stone building. I surely enjoyed the joy, rejoicing and shouts of victory. I was about twelve years old, yet I liked to see and hear them testify and praise.

Some years later a large brick church was built and a great indebtedness was made and it was a burden to pay the debt off. We remember that the shouts of victory did not continue so marked then. This has been a mistake of so many denominations.

After my sister began teaching school I worked for my board and went to school in the city at one place and my oldest brother, Edmund worked for his board at another place. We did chores for our board and room and we always got along so nicely doing the duties for the people. Our parents had taught us to work at home.

DEATH OF MOTHER

When I was 18 years old my mother died at the age of 48. She had the change of life and the doctor gave her medicine and it had an adverse effect on her (the light of healing through Jesus alone was not brought to us yet). My heart sorrowed, as did all of us six children and my father, after her death. Nobody told us Jesus bore our sorrow and carried our grief (Isa. 55:3). We knew, however, that our mother was good and we should meet her again. After this we moved to Beatrice, Nebraska. I continued my school life, entering the junior year in the high school. Soon, however, I quit school.

NIGH TO DEATH AND HEALED IN ANSWER TO PRAYER

In the winter of 1890, I was taken with the lagrippe* and pneumonia and became very ill. My folks called doctors, Mr. and Mrs. Starr and Dr. Harris. Some of them said I might live four more hours. My folks asked prayer for me and sent for the Methodist preacher, Brother Stewart, and his wife. They came quietly to me and prayed, asking God to spare my life. He told God he believed I had a greater work to do. While he was praying, I felt like God heard him. I had a wonderful experience, it seemed that I traveled the way to heaven. I just got there and came back.

My oldest sister, Elizabeth, prayed, wringing her hands over the cook stove, asking, God to heal me. I improved very fast. The doctors said it was marvelous the way I lived. My folks kept on doctoring me, but I know now, I was healed out of the doctors' hands through answer to prayer. I know, too, that I did not need the medicine and the doctor also saw this very soon.

Once that spring, I prayed all night once for my oldest brother, Edmund, and he came back to the Lord (he was at Pickering, Nebraska). My heart has believed the promise in Act 15: 30, 31, "What must I do to be saved? Believe on the Lord Jesus Christ, and thou shalt be saved, and thy house." So I believed for all our household to be saved. My oldest sister, Elizabeth, was married to Lincoln H. Paine and for some years they stood on the promises of Jesus to heal through answer to prayer. Several of their children have never tasted medicine.**

---

*Chest congestion or pneumonia

**Many early Pentecostals often refused to receive medical treatment of any kind. Some thought it was of the Devil while others only saw it as a hindrance to their faith in God to heal. Charles F. Parham taught his followers to abstain from medicinal remedies. Today, very few Pentecostals would hold to the extreme position of prohibiting doctors and medication. Ed.

BIBLE STUDY

I had joined the Y.W.C.A. and Sisters White and Sibbly gave us lessons from the Bible. As we studied the Bible with them they gave us verses on different subjects and the Scriptures were opened up to us all in a wonderful way. The subject of assurance was made so clear that no one needed to doubt about God accepting them and saving them, washing away every sin as in John 10:9, "I am the door; by me if any man enter in, he shall be saved, and shall go in and out and find pasture."

As we studied the subject of baptism I saw and felt the need of being baptized in like manner. And every honest heart will let the Word have place and desire its fulfillment. Then, by obeying the Word, we eat the Word and live by it. By the same, we are made strong.

By these Scriptures I saw I had never been baptized. My heart, was filled with a desire to obey my Lord and I gladly sought to have this ordinance fulfilled. I went to the Methodist pastor where I belonged and he tried to talk me out of being baptized by immersion, but I saw it in the Bible. He gave me verses in the Old Testament, but baptism was never taught until John and Jesus. He gave me histories that told of sprinkling, but I saw that was man's teachings and traditions of elders which was not of God.

Then, I went to the Baptist preacher and asked him to baptize me, but he would not unless I joined the Baptist church. It was not more churches I wanted; I wanted to obey the Lord as He said. Afterward, I went to the Christian Church preacher and he was willing, so I was blessed in obeying God and was baptized in the Name of the Father, the Son and the Holy Ghost. Each of us who followed Jesus in His example of baptism all went down into the water, and I know I fulfilled the command of Jesus.

The subject of the second coming of Jesus was also made real to us. Our hearts gladly responded to the call from the Word to be ready ourselves and also to preach to others.

We also saw the need of having the baptism of the Holy Spirit, to have the oil in our vessels which are our physical bodies. In many other places Jesus taught His followers and the believer their need after He left them. Their need, He emphasized, was to have power by receiving the Holy Spirit as taught further in another chapter. When He was given to one and to many others as is written. Jesus said, "And behold, I send the promise of my Father upon you; but tarry ye in the city of Jerusalem until ye be endued with power from on high. And he led them out as far as to Bethany; and He lifted up his hands and blessed them.

"And it came to pass, while he blessed them, He was parted from them and carried up into heaven. And they worshipped him and returned to Jerusalem with great joy. And were continually in the temple praising and blessing God" (Luke 24:49-53).

God's plan is given to His children that they be sealed unto the "day of redemption" (Eph. 4:30).

And also many other subjects were opened up to us as we never saw before. The truth and teaching of divine healing was made so clear that I never went back after studying it then. "Is any sick among you? Let him call for the elders of the church: and let them pray over him, anointing him with oil in the name of the Lord; and the prayer of faith shall raise him up; and if he have committed sins, they shall be forgiven. Pray one for another, that ye may be healed. The effectual fervent prayer of a righteous man availeth much" (James 5:13-16).

These promises and many others in the Old and in the New Testament taught Jesus as the healer for us today. Also God's word teaches us we may have power over the enemy, the Devil. And as we believe we have the Word fulfilled for ourselves and we do have power over all diseases and sickness and over all the power of the enemy, the devil. And, as we believe, we have the Word fulfilled for ourselves and others according to our faith so be it done unto us.

In the Y.W.C.A. we were admonished to do personal work dealing with people individually about their souls, and I only wished the Methodist Church had urged us out this way. For my heart longed to do more for my Master. I did not care for the suppers or socials.I wanted too talk to hearts about their need. And, I always felt glad to give unto Jesus without buying a supper or something else.

One afternoon, I went around and invited people to an evening service and I was almost overcome with the heat, it being a very hot day. In the evening I was dizzy and my knees were weak so I did not feel that I could walk to the meeting. I was sitting down and had thought I would have a pencil and paper brought to me and would write and tell those who were going to lead the meeting that I could not come, for I felt so badly. Just then, I heard as it were the still small voice saying, "Pray," and Jesus saying, "Trust Me." I waited on the Lord and as soon as I could believe I put my hands on my head and said, "I believe," and also on my knees I said, "I believe," and I was healed. I went to the meeting. That was the first time I knew healing power through faith and through my prayers. As I heard the truth taught it had a great place in my heart.

In the summer of 1890, I was prayed for and I have never taken medicine since. My sister Elizabeth had a child without sickness or suffering, and that encouraged my faith very much. His name is John.

BIBLE SCHOOL

My father married again and as the way was opened for me to go to Bible school, I went to St. Paul, Minnesota, to C. Horton's Bible school from 1892 to 1893. I had a severe test of diarrhoea and I prayed. I felt assured of healing and as I went I was healed. I enjoyed the mission work very much. In the fall of 1894, Brother Horton expected to go into the evangelistic work and I wished to continue in Bible school.

One day I asked God for a sign if it was His will for me to go to New York City to A. B. Simpson's Bible school. I asked for Him to have some one bring me something, saying, "Here, I give this to you." And that morning, a woman came in with a cup of hot water for my breakfast saying, "Here, I give this to you."

Through the consecrated life of Sister Carrie Markerson, who worked in a home, her employers turned to the Lord. They used wine and other extravagances on the table and for themselves, but gave them up as they saw the life she was living in self-denial, services and sacrifices for Jesus. They also gave up possessions for the Lord's work. And, as they saw a need, with glad hearts they gave unto the Lord.

Sister Carrie Markerson and I were missionary students in the same Bible class and friends, so as she had the privilege of having company, she invited me to visit her in the home where she was working, at Mr. and Mrs. Masterson's. I was there twice. They enjoyed talking about the Lord and the Lord's work. And as they knew of me going to New York City to continue the study of the Bible, they gave me of their means and were used in helping others of the Lord's servants and they will have a reward in due season as they faint not.

In the fall, my oldest sister Elizabeth and husband sent me money to come to Nebraska where they and all my folks still lived.

In October, 1904, I went to New York City by way of Chicago and stopped at the Moody Bible school three days. I realized this was a grand work.

I also stopped off at Niagara Falls for a few hours. Just across the bridge was Canada. My whole heart magnified God for the flow of His love as I took a view of the falls made by God. I had glorious seasons of prayer and praises. At the Bible school, I learned much from the Word of God as given out by His servants. Our teachers were A. B.

Simpson, Farr, Funk, Wilson and Stephen Merritt. The latter had learned much about the workings of the Holy Ghost, and our hearts were blessed as we were admonished to trust Him to use us.

I enjoyed going to the, different missions. We went regularly to the 8th Street Mission and at times to the Water Street Hadly Mission, Florence Critegan Mission and Jerry McAlley Mission. Once, a company of us went to Chinatown. As we went there we realized the awful need of every Christian being a faithful witness for Jesus.

At the Christian Mission Alliance Bible school we were privileged to bid farewell to many dear hearts who laid their lives down, going to Africa, China, India and Jerusalem.

I was asked to go to Old Orchard, Maine, with an older lady. She offered to pay one half of my fare. We went on the ship from New York City to Boston. God's love in breadth, width and depth was realized as we viewed the ocean. Oh, glory! It was a beautiful sight and a wonderful experience for me. We traveled by night both ways, and had some opportunities to witness for Jesus. The meeting of the convention was a grand one to my soul.

Later, I came to Wayerly, New York. There were five of us girls in the mission work. One, Miss Celia Williams, was taken very sick. Her companion, Miss Jennie Sampson, and I were by her bedside and Jennie said to me, "She is not breathing." I felt in faith for her healing and did not turn to look. It seemed that I would doubt by looking. Soon she began to breath and sang with a strong voice. In a short time she gave out the message in power. This has strengthened my faith many times.

Some years later a chapel was built there in a wonderful way by trusting the Lord. A lot was obtained and some work and a little material donated. The men went to work with what was at hand and God added to and supplied the need for the entire building. I always referred to it as a faith building.

Praying one time to know God's will, an angel appeared at my side and I reached out my hand to touch it and it vanished.

The Lord made it clear to me to go to Elmira, New York, and as I was looking to the Lord to supply the money I received a letter from the sister who went with me to Maine. She sent me the money and fulfilled her promise she had made. I had great faith in her and felt the need of her and every one keeping their word and promises. If we make a vow or make a promise we should be very careful to keep the vow and fulfill our promise.

I went back to Nebraska, at the request and provision of my oldest sister, Elizabeth. I stopped at Alexander Dowie's divine healing home. I had him pray for me, for I had chills and night sweats. As soon as he prayed, he said, "She is touched or she is healed." I was delivered and I have never had that since. Bless God.

Dowie declared the Word in power at that time. It was before he had entered into the error he afterward took up. I shall never forget one sermon he preached from the text, "The power of the Lord was present to heal them" (Luke 5:17). During a service a cloud of glory, as it looked, was all over him and only his head could be seen. Some were marvelously healed there.

My youngest sister, Mary Ella Ozman, gave up her life as a missionary. She went to Bible school at Kansas City for some time. As she heard God's call to the foreign field, she gave her life to go and was called to go to South America. She went in 1901, in the summer. She was happy in laying down her life for the Indian people there. She lived a happy Christian life all her days.

Mary died in 1903. She lies at rest in South America until the resurrection day. After she departed, the nationals said, who now would come and read to them and give them attention? Mary was with Sister Anderson, who was in South America some years.

I had the same test and temptation to sorrow as at the time of mother's death, but the comfort of Jesus was revealed to my heart in such a peaceful and powerful way by having the Holy Ghost within. Jesus said, "He is with you and shall be in you."

Once in a meeting while at Lincoln, Nebraska, I was asked to talk in a missionary meeting and the remembrance of Mary's death came up to me with such grief I thought, "I cannot be up before the people." At once the comfort of the Holy Spirit was given me and I led the services in victory. In the natural it would have been hard, since it was near the time of her passing.

Before the way was opened for me to go out of my home city of Beatrice, the Lord permitted me to have the use of an empty house in a needy part of the city. A meeting was held for children and God blessed a number. Many needy hearts were visited and my own soul was satisfied in doing this little for Jesus.

KANSAS CITY, KANSAS AND MISSOURI

I spent some time in missionary work at Kansas City and I called on a sick woman. She became very bad and the doctors called the family, saying she was dying. She looked up and asked me to lay hands on her and pray. I did so, according to Mark 16:18, "They shall lay hands on the sick, and they shall recover." She was healed and said she felt something like electricity go through her.

Another woman had bowel trouble, using pills or syringes, and she asked me to lay hands on her and pray. After prayer she said she was healed and used nothing and took no more medicine. All glory to Jesus' Name. The Bible fulfilled, blessed our hearts.

I became acquainted with Sister Van Noi of Kansas City and she asked me to pray for God to give her His deliverance at childbirth so she would not have any pain and I asked God for the miracle. She had no sickness, no pain at the birth of the child. Oh, how we bless our God for He is just the same to the holy women of today as the Bible records. We declare this marvelous deliverance and do testify to its fulfillment to spare some mothers from temptations in hindering God's plan in giving life, and save some others from destroying life when God has put seed in to bring forth.

I also have a personal testimony of the marvelous deliverance God gave me at the birth of the only child He gave us when I was 41 years old. It was without sickness or pain and I had neither doctor nor medicine.

TOPEKA, KANSAS, BIBLE SCHOOL

The Bible school was opened at Bethel College in October 1901. I asked the Lord to give me the fare if it was His will for me to go there and one sister gave me $5.00 and soon afterwards she gave me the same amount again. I felt assured it was from the hand of God. I, with a number of others went from Kansas City.

We studied the Bible, attended a mission in the city of Topeka and did some visiting in homes. We, the students, did the work of the house and we were blessed, doing the most humble service unto Jesus, as we had been taught to do. "And whatsoever ye do in word or deed, do all in the name of the Lord Jesus, giving thanks to God and the Father by him" (Col. 3: 17).

It was proclaimed and preached that God had a mighty outpouring and baptism of the Holy Ghost and power for His people everywhere and that it was our privilege to have it fulfilled to us here and now. At first, and for a time, I held to the experiences I had had in praises, joy, answers to prayer and seeing the sick healed as the Baptism of the Spirit. Soon, however, I was convinced of a need within. For about three weeks my heart became hungry for, the baptism of the Holy Ghost. I wanted the promise of the Father more than I wanted food or sleep.

On New Year's night, January 1, 1901, near eleven o'clock, I asked that prayer be offered for me and hands be laid on me to fulfill all scripture, that I might receive the baptism which my whole heart longed to have. There as I was praying I remembered in the Bible hands were laid on believers as on me and prayer was offered for me.

I began to talk in tongues and had great joy and was filled with glory. After this fulfillment of promise as in Acts 19:1-6, others in the school became hungry for this outpouring and three days after the Baptism of the Holy Ghost came in me, He was received by twelve others, each one spoke in tongues. Some had the interpretation also and when the language was spoken it was translated into English and was all was edifying.

I did not know that I would talk with tongues when I received the baptism, but as soon as I received on that night, I spoke in tongues. I knew I had received the promise of the Father, fulfilled. Blessed be God! There came, such a joy and fullness of the presence of the Lord in me. I never knew such a presence before. In the morning of the 2nd of January different ones asked me about the outpouring I had received the night before. God poured out His Spirit upon me so mightily and so wonderfully and when I began to talk I spoke in tongues. I motioned for paper and pencil and when I started to write I did not write in English, but made characters in another language. Afterwards, I opened the Bible in Acts and read about the experiences God gave them and how He had this same mighty outpouring for us today. This was the fulfillment of the promise for which we had been praying.

On studying the account in Joel 2:23, it reads, "He will cause to come down for you the rain, the former and the latter rain in the first *month*." While "month" is in italics, yet it was fulfilled to us in being poured out in the first month with us in Topeka and when the Lord gave the outpouring in Los Angeles it was in April, which was the first month in the Jewish year. In Acts, as recorded, was the former rain of the Spirit.

Soon, it was noised abroad that a strange thing happened at the Bethel College. There was a piece put in the daily paper at Topeka about "talking in strange tongues" as they called it. Other editors in Kansas City and St. Louis read it and came to see us. We conversed with them about this experience and told how we prayed for the Baptism of the Holy Ghost and God poured out His power on us and then we spoke in those languages. While talking to the newspaper men, some of the students spoke in tongues as they were explaining the experience.

These men also wanted my photograph, for I was the first one to receive the baptism in the school. First I objected, and then they insisted, saying they would take a snapshot any way. Finally, I decided it would do me no hurt and I gave them one of my photos and let them take it. It all came out in the papers about the strange tongues spoken at the Bethel College. This only spread abroad the works of God and some hungry hearts came to Topeka. Others wrote to us, inquiring about the way. So we blessed God and gave thanks for all things.

We made a study of the outpouring of the Holy Ghost and found the sign given when the former rain of the Spirit was poured out was talking in tongues and magnifying Jesus. "And they were all filled with the Holy Spirit, and began to speak with other tongues as the Spirit had given them utterance" (Acts 2:4).

In another text, we read, "While Peter yet spake these words, the Holy Ghost fell on all them which heard the Word. And they of the circumcision which believed were astonished as many as came with Peter, because that on the Gentiles also was poured out the gift of the Holy Spirit for they heard them speak with tongues and magnify God" (Acts 10: 44-46).

Again, we read concerning the 12 Ephesian believers in Acts 19, "And when Paul had laid his hands upon them the Holy Ghost came on them; and they spake with tongues, and prophesied" (Acts 19:6).

And now, God is pouring out the latter rain of the Spirit, and He is restoring the gifts and power to believers. Further, God is sealing the Bride with His Spirit.

Reading the Bible, we learn that Mary the mother of Jesus and other women were present in the Acts account and that they tarried for the promise of the Father and received the baptism of the Holy Ghost. That is a great encouragement to the women that God is baptizing today. We know the God who gave the languages spoken in those women is living today.

At the first outpouring every man heard them "speak in his own language" (Acts 2:6). And the different nationalities, some seventeen as are named, were present and said, "We do hear them speak in our tongue the wonderful works of God" (Acts 2:11).

The next night after I received the Holy Ghost, I believe it was, I, with others, went to a mission down town in Topeka. My heart was full of glory and blessings. I began to pray in English and then in tongues. At the close of the services a man who is a Bohemian said he understood what I said in his own language. At other times, many of those who have heard have known the language. Even a government interpreter and foreigners have understood the tongues as languages they knew.

In Acts 2:12, they said, "What meaneth this?" They did not understand how these Galileans could speak their own language. When my husband first heard speaking in tongues at a street meeting in Oklahoma City, Oklahoma, two women spoke in tongues and he thought they had learned the language they were speaking. It was a sign to him, and it made him hungry. At other times he heard others speak in tongues and he followed them to their mission where he came back to the Lord.

In the summer of 1910, he left his trade as a carpenter, rented a tent and attended the Pentecostal camp meetings. He tarried until he received the Holy Ghost and he spoke in tongues and had added freedom and power.

The third day he, with Brother Hatcher and others, received the Holy Spirit. He, like Paul, fell to the ground before he received the Spirit and was greatly blessed. When he fell, he arose talking in tongues. No wonder, others mocking said, "These are full of new wine."

When the Holy Ghost was given at Topeka, Kansas, some of them fell under the power and were filled so that we could hardly stand up. We shouted, lifting our hands and talking in tongues. Many times we could only talk in other languages.

A company of twenty of us baptized men and women from Topeka, Kansas, went to Lawrence, Kansas, in the spring of 1901 and held a meeting. We went by twos over the city, calling and praying for people. Meetings were held every night in an old theatre. There were many good results, some were saved, the sick were healed, and a number received the Holy Ghost and spoke in tongues.

Sister Fannie Dobson, now of Yellsville, Arkansas, received the baptism, speaking in tongues while we were in Lawrence. She is still standing true to the work. Sister Waldron also tarried and had the promise fulfilled.

Later, we went to Des Moines, Iowa, declaring the Word as it is written. Brother Howard Stanley of 1308 W. Gordon Street, North Topeka, Kansas, had a blessed experience at the Bible school, speaking in tongues much and interpreting. Many of his father's house received the Holy Ghost and were used there. He also visited Kansas City and God baptized a number with the Holy Ghost in that city, saving and healing the sick.

A company of us lifted up Jesus in a school house; I began to pray in English and then the Holy Ghost prayed in tongues and a Bohemian said I spoke in his language. Workers went over to Kansas, Missouri, Texas and other states declaring the Word as it is written. God honored His Word and poured out His Spirit on hungry hearts.

We heard Brother Seymour in the tabernacle at Houston, Texas where the Holy Ghost had been poured out mightily. He had the light of the baptism when in Texas and was praying for its fulfillment. Parties hearing of the Holy Ghost being given here, sent him money to come to

Los Angeles, California. They supposed he had its fulfillment, but he received it later.

Seymour went to Los Angeles, California, and meetings were started and as hungry hearts prayed, God mightily poured out the Holy Ghost. Many received the Holy Spirit and spoke in tongues and great joy and glory was given.

On the evening of April 9, 1906, on Bonnie Brey [Brae, *Ed.*] Street the Spirit first fell in Los Angeles. Afterwards because of the need for more room, they moved to the Azusa Street Mission at 312 Azusa Street. Men and women came there from all over the world and now have this fulfillment of promise. There are missionaries in the foreign fields who have the promise of the Holy Ghost now and are having signs following as it is written.

Jesus Christ, before His ascension, commanded His apostles to tarry in Jerusalem for the promise of the Father. He told them they would receive power when the Holy Ghost came upon them. The apostles obeyed those instructions, going to the upper room and waiting. They did not wait a little while and then decide to claim the Holy Ghost by faith. They expected what every believer has a right to expect today, to be really filled with the Holy Spirit.

Acts 2:4 describes their experience, "And they were all filled with the Holy Spirit, and began to speak with other tongues, as the Spirit gives utterance." Notice it says they were all filled. It does not say they were blessed, felt happy, that their emotions were stirred, or that after the experience they felt more love or had more liberty in testimony, preaching or prayer. It says they were all filled with the Holy Ghost.

Now when they were filled with the Holy Spirit they at once began to speak in tongues as the Spirit gave them utterance. If then, this was the sign which God chose to give to His apostles and to each of those that assembled in the upper room (which was about one hundred and twenty and included the mother of Jesus and the other women) and on the other occasions as related when His Spirit came upon them and into them, is it a mistake to believe that He would give us the same sign when we receive the same blessed experience they received?

Now if this sign had only followed in the one instance we would hardly feel free to declare it to be the evidence of the baptism, or that it must necessarily follow in all cases. But, in the three recorded instances where the Spirit was poured out in the days of the apostles, it is clearly stated in these cases that this same sign followed, and in the fourth instance it is clearly implied. In Acts 8:17 Simon the sorcerer, who witnessed the scene, was so moved by what he saw that he at once tried to buy the power to impart the Holy Ghost in the same manner.

How sad it is to see men robbing themselves and others of God's real gift of the Holy Ghost by trying to explain away these wonderful Scriptures which so clearly set forth God's one way of bestowing this priceless gift on true believers on the Lord Jesus Christ, as in Acts 10:44.

How long will men and women be satisfied with their theories and refuse to humble their hearts and tarry until the blessed Holy Spirit comes upon them and fills them, taking possession of their entire beings and speaking through them in other tongues, thus proving to all that the Holy Ghost is a real, living person and that they have received Him according to the Scriptures rather than holding to some theory of men.

In Acts 19:6 is laid down the Bible way of God's children dealing with believers who want the gift of the Holy Ghost. This text also gives the evidence they had when receiving. This same sign and evidence is following the believers who receive the gift of the Holy Spirit throughout the United States and over the world today.

Believers in all the countries of the heathen world are receiving the same Holy Spirit with the same mighty sign of talking in tongues since the Holy Spirit was given some of us in January, 1901. At that time the baptism was first given in a continuous way and is given unto this day, here and elsewhere.

On this June 23, 1920, one was praying and praising God and he was heard to speak as the Spirit gave utterance in other tongues. He told us he received the Holy Spirit and he felt God's great power "come in." He had been converted a few days ago and so he came hungry for all God had for him. Our souls feast with those who tarry until they are endued with power from on high.

What more can one say but as God says, "The promise is unto you and your children and unto them that are afar off, even as many as the Lord our God shall call."

*This article was taken from pages 7-39 of the book **What God Hath Wrought** by Agnes N.Ozman LaBerge. The book was originally published in 1921. The story, as it appears here, has undergone serious editing and in several instances sentences have been paraphrased. The editing was done both to abridge and clarify the text. This editing has in no instance changed the historical record as remembered by LaBerge. Other editorial changes could be made and no doubt some would make the text more acceptable to those readers who are concerned about proper grammar and style. The editor has tried, however, to preserve LaBerge's original writing style, even when tempted to make changes that might improve it.*

A specimen of Agnes Ozman's "inspired"
handwriting.
The Topeka Daily Capital
January 6, 1901
(Public Domain)

Chapter 8

A COLLECTION OF PERIODICAL ARTICLES

By Various Authors

**A QUEER FAITH
STRANGE ACTIONS OF THE APOSTOLIC BELIEVERS
ARE INSPIRED FROM GOD.
THE BELIEVERS SPEAK A STRANGE LANGUAGE AND
WRITE A PECULIAR HAND--S.J. RIGGINS
EXTRAORDINARY STATEMENT.**

There are great goings on at the old mansion in the southwestern part of town known as "Stone's Folly." If the statement of S.J. Riggins, a young convert of the Apostolic Faith is to be believed.

Mr. Riggins is a young man who came here from Kansas City about the 31st of October to join the "Apostolic Congregation" which is presided over and was founded in this section by Charles F. Parham. Mr. Parham, it will be remembered, was a student at the Apostolic school at Shiloh, Me. which gained so much prominence lately when Lizzie

Bell, the young Topeka girl wandered away from the school in a fit of temporary insanity. A posse of officers scoured the country for days until she was found, in a weak condition, and taken care of.

Parham led a colony to this Maine school from Kansas City and Topeka traveling overland to the New England town and holding gospel meetings on the way. Miss Bell went with this colony of religious enthusiasts. Parham afterwards returned to Topeka and started a "school" or "congregation" at the old Stone mansion in the southwestern part of this city, near Seabrook.

The "congregation" at present numbers thirty-five persons and they certainly form a strange religious body. Most of the thirty-five members are from Kansas City--coming here with Mr. Parham--but a few are from Topeka.

It seems that under the Apostolic faith its adherents are prevented from asking for money contributions except through God himself. They believe that the Lord answers prayer and they pray incessantly for what they want, giving little heed to the present, practical need of making a living. Most of the members took all their earthly possessions to the "mansion" with them and these possessions are being slowly absorbed for living expenses. According to Mr. Riggins, a man named Stanley, a convert to the faith, as well as his family, brought over $100 worth of furniture when the mansion was rented. Mr. Stanley owns a farm southwest of town and, according to Mr. Riggins, he is about to sacrifice this to keep the "school" going.

The several persons who are members of the "school" all live in the mansion. It is fitted up into apartments and here the families dwell. Their daily duties are few. The food is to be cooked and there is the care of a single cow which furnishes milk for the whole colony.

The whole day is spent with prayer, for be it known that these adherents to an exacting creed believe that prayer and faith bring inspiration direct form God Himself, and when they arrive at a certain stage of perfection they have all the qualifications and attributes of the apostles of old.

The leader, Parham, claims to be an apostle from God and there are several members who claim to be endowed with power from on high.

But the really strange feature of the faith is the so called "gift of tongues from heaven." When this is received after long continued prayer, the members who succeed in getting it talk to each other in a sort of senseless gibberish and write a strange system of shorthand or hieroglyphics, which they say is conveyed from God personally.

The original "gift of tongues from heaven" woman in this "congregation," according to Mr. Riggins, is a Miss Auswin [Agnes Ozman, *Ed.*], a specimen of whose handwriting while under the spell is given with this article.

Last Friday afternoon at 3 o'clock the members of the congregation started on a long session of prayer. They kept it up without ceasing until Saturday morning at 3:30 and then, according to Mr. Riggins' story, there were about twelve of them jabbering a strange gibberish at once, they said was the voice of God through them.

"I believe the whole of them are crazy," said Mr. Riggins to a **Capital** reporter. "I never saw anything like it." They were racing about the room talking and gesticulating and using this strange and senseless language which they claim is the word from the Most High."

"I believe in a portion of the Apostolic faith," said Mr. Riggins earnestly. "But I could not subscribe to it in its entirety and so left the congregation.

"I do not believe their senseless jargon means anything. I am trying to be an earnest Christian. I have left the 'school' without money to pay my fare to go anywhere, although I have a place of lodging. I have no home and I am determined to study for the ministry and I have faith in God that he will provide a way. I do not claim to be an apostle and my whole desire is to do good in an humble capacity. When I left the 'congregation' today, I told why I did so, with all the earnestness at my command."

Mr. Riggins said that some of Miss Auswin's writing, which she claimed to be inspired, was submitted to a Chinaman here in Topeka with the honest intention of seeing if he could translate it. The Celestial threw up his hand and said: "Me no understand. Takee to Jap."*

Mr. Riggins told this story without a suspicion of levity and if he put any humor in it at the last it was done unconsciously, for he seemed terribly in earnest.

*This article first appeared in the **Topeka Daily Capital** on January 6, 1901.*

• • • • • • • • • • •

ROW AT BETHEL.
S.J. RIGGINS WITHDRAWS FROM PARHAM SCHOOL
TAKES NO STOCK IN RECENT "GIFT OF TONGUES."
STRANGE GIBBERISH
"STUDENTS" TALK BUT NO ONE UNDERSTANDS THEM.
MR. PARHAM CALLS IT "POWER OF THE LORD."

There is a row at Bethel Bible college. S.J. Riggins, a student, is the cause of the trouble. He pronounces the institution a "fake" of the most pronounced type. This is the school at the Stone mansion west of the city, founded by Rev. Charles F. Parham and which he is conducting on faith principles.

Mr. Parham and his followers believe they have the gift of tongues spoken of in the second chapter of the Acts of the Apostles. With this they have the power of discernment and the gift of prophecy.

Mr. Riggins came to the school several weeks ago with a class from Kansas City. He went there, as he says, "to study the Bible and do what I could for the cause of

---

*This language, although considered appropriate when this was written, may be offensive today. It has been printed only to convey the original message, not to offend.

God, but there were those at the school whom I did not think were the earnest Christians I had supposed them to be; and I left the school to work in the city and study the Bible. Later I went to Kansas City and worked with one of the missions there, and afterwards came back to Bethel. This was after the ones with whom I could not work had left.

"After studying at the school the last time things I came to a pretty pass. They began to claim the gift of tongues and the gift of discernment, and each talked a different kind of gibberish, claiming to be inspired by God, and that they talked one of the foreign languages.

"I was not under the influence, and could see that the students of the school had been led to this extreme through their fanaticism, and finally decided to leave the school. Accordingly, last Saturday morning I went away but before going I called the inmates of the building together and explained to them my reasons for leaving. I told them they were under the influence of the evil one and that the best they could do would be to leave the school, as I was doing. They all laughed at me, and I left the school, and do not intend to return."

The Bible school was started at Stone's Folly some months ago by Mr. Parham, who for several years has been the pastor of the Apostolic congregation in this city. He was brought into some prominence last fall through being connected for a time with Rev. Sandborn, who took a class of about sixty to his Bible school at Shiloh, Me., among them being Lizzie Bell, the Topeka girl who ran away from the school during an alleged fit of temporary insanity.

After returning from Shiloh, Me., Mr. Parham shortly after started the Bible school in this city, which is conducted on the lines laid down by the larger school at Shiloh.

Theirs is a faith belief, and it is through faith and prayer that the school is kept in existence. Everything used at the school has been furnished through free-will offering and in answer to prayer. It is their belief that everything needed by them will be furnished them through divine influence. Their faith also teaches healing prayer.

About a week ago the "gift of tongues" was bestowed upon one of their number, Miss Agnes N. Ozman, who began to speak in words which it is claimed is one of the foreign languages. Since that time she has written and spoken several languages it is claimed through inspiration of God.

About fifteen members of the colony have now been given the gift of tongues and when a **State Journal** reporter called at the school this morning each of the favored ones were called up and spoke a few sentences in strange and unnatural way outlandish words which they neither know the meaning of nor the language to which they belonged. Their reason for uttering them is that the Lord inspires them and that during the time they are speaking they do not know what they are saying, but afterwards the Lord prompts them to utter the meaning of the strange words.

It is a peculiar sight to see a whole room full of the men and women of the school sitting around, occasionally breaking out with brief outbursts of talk in one of the many languages which they claim to speak, and writing the quaint and indistinguishable hieroglyphics which they believe to be the characters for words in the Syrian, Chinese, Japanese, Arabic and other languages.

Mr. Parham said, "It is a wonderful work coming as it does on the eve of the twentieth century. We have for long believed that the power of the Lord would be manifested in our midst, and that power would be given us to speak other languages, and that the time will come when we will be sent to go into all the nations and preach the gospel, and that the Lord will give us the power of speech to talk to the people of the various nations without having to study them in school."

*This article was originally published in the **Topeka State Journal**, January 7, 1901.*

• • • • • • • • • • •

HINDOO [HINDU. Ed.] AND ZULU
BOTH ARE REPRESENTED AT BETHEL SCHOOL
"GIFT OF TONGUES" CONTINUES AT THE
FAITH COLLEGE
STRANGE THINGS SEEN
STUDENTS SUDDENLY BEGIN TALKING IN STRANGE
LANGUAGES
THEY CAN NOT EVEN UNDERSTAND THEMSELVES

Religious excitement still prevails at Bethel college, in spite of the desertion of S.J. Riggins and the "gift of tongues" continues.

It now has been about two weeks since "the gift" was first bestowed upon Miss Agnes N. Ozman. The students, of which there are 40, take the Bible for their only text book. They sit around the building in various attitudes reading the Bible nearly all the time. The work of the school such as keeping the building in repairs, attending to the barn and grounds, keeping house, and cooking the meals is done by the students, each doing a share. This however is not sufficient to occupy the time of any of the students for long and the remainder is spent in reading the Bible.

The classes are conducted by Mr. Parham. There are no regular stated times when the classes are held but whenever one is called the members of the class assemble in the chapel and take turns reading a verse aloud. As each verse is read some little time is spent in discussing it and deciding upon its meaning.

Recently the class has been studying in the book of Acts and the twelfth chapter is devoted to a list of things, the doing of which are accredited to the Apostles. Among the things mentioned is the power of discernment, the gift of tongues and the gift of prophecy.

It has been the desire of the students that they be given the gift of tongues so that they might be thus enabled to go as missionaries to foreign countries without first having to pass a term in some school to learn the language of the natives of the country to which they wish to go. Accordingly they went to their Lord in prayer and asked that this gift of tongues might be bestowed upon them.

The students were in real earnest in their pleadings in this direction and the first intimation they had that their prayers were to be answered was when Miss Ozman, one of the students who came here from Kansas City went off into what was apparently a trance and began to utter strange words, the like of which had never been heard by her listeners before.

She afterward gave the following explanation: "The Lord inspired me with the words and I did not know at the time I was talking, what the next word I uttered would be. I do not know what language I was talking nor what I was saying only as the Lord would inspire me."

Rev. Mr. Parham said: "The matter went on for nearly a week before the gift was bestowed upon others. All the while the students were praying to their utmost that the gift could be theirs. Finally several of the others were favored with the gift and now there are about 15 or 20 of the students who sit around and occasionally burst out talking a lot of sentences unintelligible to those who hear it and not understood by those who speak it until told the meaning by inspiration of God."

When a **State Journal** reporter called at the building to see the founder and leader of the school, Mr. Parham he was shown into what was apparently a common sitting room on the first floor. Several men were in the room, each reading a Bible. Miss Ozman sat at a desk writing some letters which were to be posted that morning. Shortly after finishing the letters she sat down to write and again and immediately announced that her hands utterly refused to write the characters of the English language. And with her hands unconsciously formed the characters of some language, but she was not able to state which. She did not interpret the marks.

In writing the characters, the muscles of Miss Ozman's hands seem to contract and she made the marks in a spasmodic fashion, her hand rather jerking back and forth to make the scrawls.

Mr. Parham has had the gift of tongues also. He says he is inspired to speak in the German language. Soon after the reporter began talking to him he was constrained to utter a few sentences in German. Soon afterward Mr. Parham spoke another language. This time it seemed to be in the Swedish language.

Samuel Higgins entered the school almost two weeks ago and has been given "the gift." He says that he speaks the Zulu language. He said: "I do not know many of the words yet but they are coming to me." He spoke a few words which he said were of that language.

Mr. Parham called Miss Lilian Thistlethrate [Thistlethwaite. *Ed.*] into the room and asked her if she could talk some. She at first answered that the Lord had not inspired her to say anything but soon began to utter strange words which sounded like this: "Euossa, Euossa, use rela sema calah mala kanah leulla ssage nalan. Ligle logle lazle logle. Ene mine mo, sah rah el me sah rah me." These sentences were translated as meaning, "Jesus is mighty to save," "Jesus is ready to hear," and "God is love."

A student known as "Brother" Howard was called in and asked to speak in his language. He spoke in the language of the East Indians, the Hindoos, it was explained. His speech seemed in the nature of a sermon and was accompanied with gestures and motions of the arm and head.

*This article was published in the **Topeka State Journal** on January 9, 1901.*

• • • • • • • • • • •

MISSIONARY WORK

Students of Bethel "College" started off on a tour of the United States yesterday afternoon. The Rev. Charles

F. Parham, leader of Bethel College assumed command of a party of seven and began a tour of the United States and Canada. It is a missionary tour. They expect to secure a long list of converts to the new faith that enables the students of talk in every language known and some that are not.

It is not improbable that Topeka has heard the last about the college and the strange "gift" which its students were miraculously given. Accompanying Rev. Mr. Parham are: Mrs. Parham, Miss Lilian Thistlethwaite, Miss Agnes Ozman, Miss Maude Stanley, Howard Stanley and Albert Horr. Last night the party stopped in Kansas city where they are praying for transportation to the next town.

*This article was published in the **Topeka Daily Capital** on January 22, 1901.*

• • • • • • • • • • •

NEW SECT IN KANSAS SPEAKS WITH STRANGE TONGUES
BETHEL GOSPEL SCHOOL AT TOPEKA,
THE MEMBERS OF WHICH "TOIL NOT NEITHER DO THEY SPIN"
PREACH NEW DOCTRINE

Topeka, Kan., Jan 25. Special Correspondence of the **Sunday Post-Dispatch**.

Strange, indeed, seem the ways of the forty men and women who compose the Bethel Gospel School, a company of religious enthusiasts, which was organized last September. They toil not, neither do they spin, neither take thought of their raiment, yet they are clothed, fed and kept warm, they claim, through faith and prayer. Moreover, they speak in strange tongues, some of which they themselves cannot understand.

When asked to explain the latter phenomenon they refer the questioner to St. Mark's Gospel, chapter 16, verse 17, which says, "And these signs shall follow them that believe: In My name they shall cast our devils; they shall speak with new tongues."

The founder of this strange sect is Charles Parham, a small man, with peculiar looking dark eyes, an auburn beard and dark hair. He leased for two years the property west of Washburn College, near this city, known as "Stone's Folly," and there set up his colony.

This property is a pretentious country house, built after the style of a feudal castle. It was erected by an eccentric man named Stone, who put all of his money into it and was unable to maintain the place. It is three stories high and contains 30 rooms. The reception hall cost $7,000, but it is ornate, rather than beautiful. The large room designed for a library is now used by the new apostles, as they consider themselves, as a chapel, and there strange scenes are nightly witnessed.

There is a praying tower, which commands a view of the city, and in this tower there is a continuous prayer, night and day. One apostle, or student, as they are sometimes called, prays until he is tired and then is relieved by another.

On New Year's Eve Miss Ozman, one of the apostles, became suddenly gifted with a new tongue and spoke in a language unknown to herself or the other members of the colony. When it was all over she had no idea what she had said.

Mr. Parham went to town the next Friday, and when he returned he found the whole crowd of apostles sitting on the floor of the parlor jabbering in strange tongues, no two speaking the same language, apparently, and on one understanding his or his neighbor's speech.

From that time on the development was marvelous. Now these apostles write by what they call inspiration in characters that are fearfully and wonderfully made, and which resemble no handwriting known to anybody in these parts.

One there is Miss Thistlethwaite, a sister-in-law of Mr. Parham, on whom they claim the gift has been bestowed more bounteously than upon any of the others, for to her has been given the ability to interpret what she speaks in foreign tongues. Her appearance is intelligent and her manner refined.

It is claimed by these students or apostles, that when any member of the colony speaks in a strange tongue, the others can plainly see the cloven tongue of fire descend upon him, exactly as they descended upon the disciples of Jesus on the Day of Pentecost.

Mr. Parham says that during the last few weeks these apostles have spoken in French, German, Swedish, Bohemian, Chinese, Japanese, Hungarian, Bulgarian, Russian, Italian, Spanish and Norwegian.

It is Parham's intention to send forth students into the world, to preach to other Gospel missions the usefulness [uselessness, *Ed.*] of preparing for foreign missionary work in the usual way, by laborious study of the languages, when by simple faith they can be acquired in an hour.

Students are preparing now for the journey, though they have no visible means of support, and are confident that money will materialize.

On Thanksgiving day and Christmas the apostles prayed for good dinners, says Mr. Parham and their prayers were answered.

He had $2 in his pocket the day before New Year's, he says, and about sixty people who had assembled from the surrounding country were to be lodged and fed. He started to town, remarking to his wife, "These people shall be entertained, even though it breaks up Bethel School."

By the time he reached Topeka, he says, he had $6. After making his purchase and returning home he still had $5 and on the day after the New Year's feast he had $35.

One night, he says, while he was praying in meeting, he felt something fall into his lap. It proved to be a purse containing $50.

One of the latest manifestations of power on the part of this strange people is that frequently, in the midst of services, they break up, not only in foreign languages, but in strange music, which none of them has ever heard before.

This article was published in the **St. Louis Post-Dispatch** *on January 25, 1901.*

• • • • • • • • • • •

PARHAM'S NEW RELIGION PRACTICED AT "STONE'S FOLLY"
EVANGELIST WHO RECENTLY ATTRACTED ATTENTION IN KANSAS CITY HAS ESTABLISHED A GOSPEL SCHOOL IN AN OLD MANSION IN TOPEKA, WHERE HE TEACHES FORTY STUDENTS HIS
STRANGE DOCTRINES--
CONVERTS GET WHAT THEY PRAY FOR, AND, BY AN INSPIRATION, SPEAK IN LANGUAGES UNKNOWN TO THEMSELVES--THE TOWER OF
CONTINUOUS PRAYER

Topeka, Kan., Jan. 25--The Rev. Charles Parham, evangelist, who recently attracted some attention in Kansas City is at the head of a company of enthusiasts who have founded what is known as the Bethel Gospel school in this city. They have leased the property known as Stone's Folly, and there they practice a new and startling kind of religion. There are forty students in the school. They pray for what they get, and get what they pray for. They do no work, yet they have plenty to eat and wear. They say the Lord provides. The school was established last September, and since that time only one student has quit--a man who declared that Parham and his followers were fanatics and that their scheme of human redemption had nothing to rest on.

In a conversation with **The Times** correspondent recently, Mr. Parham said that on New Year's day one of the students, Miss Ozman, became suddenly gifted with a new and strange tongue, and spoke in a language unknown to herself or the others, and knew not what she said. "The next day," said Parham, "I went to town, and upon my return found all the students sitting on the floor talking in unknown tongues, no two talking the same language, and no one understanding his or his neighbor's speech. From that time on the spiritual development was marvelous for the students now are able to write by inspiration."

Parham says that the gift has been bestowed upon his sister-in-law, Miss Thistlethwaite, more bounteously than upon the others. She is able to interpret what she says in an unknown tongue "Whenever any student speaks in an unknown tongue," says Parham, "the other students can see the cloven tongue of fire descend upon the speaker."

Parham asserts that the students--all Americans without education in foreign languages--have lately spoken in French, German, Swedish, Bohemian, Chinese, Japanese, Hungarian, Bulgarian, Russian, Italian, Spanish and Norwegian.

"We have received several messages to go into all the world and preach the gospel," said Mr. Parham, "and we must obey the command. A part of our labor will be to teach the churches the uselessness of spending years of time preparing missionaries for work in foreign lands when all they have to do is to ask God for power and then have faith that the power will come."

"All things come though faith," Mr. Parham continued. "We ask God for food and raiment and we receive them. I have started out many a day without a cent and returned with $25; my prayers had been answered. There was nothing supernatural about it. I needed the money for the Lord's work; He knew it, and put it into the hearts of men who had money to supply my wants. I needed a turkey for my students on Christmas; I prayed for it; my prayer was answered; a farmer's wife sent us a turkey. We wanted power from on high to help save the world; we prayed for it; we received it."

Stone's Folly, where the Parham school is conducted, was built several years ago by an eccentric old man named Stone. He never lived in it, and the property was unoccupied until Parham leased it. The house cost $40,000. It is built on the order of an old feudal castle, three full stories, with thirty rooms. The drawing room is used by the students for a chapel. A tower which commands a fine view of the city and surrounding country is known as the praying tower. Prayer in the tower is continuous night and day, the students relieving each other.

Parham and his wife, Miss Ozman and Miss Thistlethwaite are quite intelligent, they wear clothes which fit, and have the appearance of people who frequent the bath; but the others of the "family" as Parham calls them, are about as tacky looking outfit as one would see in a trip around the world. They may be clean spiritually, but physically they are anything but shining marks of cleanliness.

A great many people visit Stone's Folly, and occasionally a visitor will seek to "argue" with Parham. When the unknown tongue is disputed. Parham always cites the 17th verse, 16th chapter of Mark, which says, "And these signs shall follow them that believe. In my name shall they cast out devils; they shall speak with new tongues."

While Parham and half a dozen of his band are in Kansas City teaching the new doctrine, thirty or more students are at Stone's Folly, praying for them.

*This article was published in the **Kansas City Times** on January 27, 1901. Much of the article was used for the following essay.*

• • • • • • • • • • •

**NEW RELIGION "DISCOVERED" AT "STONE'S FOLLY"
NEAR TOPEKA**

The "discovery" of a new religion, or perhaps as its devotees claim, the recovery of that which was lost, has been made, and in Kansas, of course. The Rev. Charles Parham claims to be the discoverer, and has established a school where the new faith is practiced. It is called the Bethel gospel school and is located at "Stone's Folly" near Topeka. Forty enthusiasts are following Parham in his new faith. They pray for what they get, and get what they pray for. They do no work, yet they have plenty to eat and wear. They say the Lord provides. The school was established last September, and since that time only one student has quit--a man who declared that Parham and his followers were fanatics and that their scheme of human redemption had nothing to rest on.

Parham declares that on New Year's day one of the students, a Miss Ozman, became suddenly gifted with a strange tongue, and spoke in a language unknown to herself or the others, and knew not what she said. "The next day," said Parham, "I went to town, and upon my return found all the students sitting on the floor talking in unknown tongues, no two talking the same language, and no one understanding his or his neighbor's speech. From that time on the spiritual development was marvelous for the students now are able to write by inspiration."

Parham says that the gift has been bestowed upon his sister-in-law, Miss Thistlethwaite, more bounteously than upon the others. She is able to interpret what she says in an unknown tongue. "Whenever any student speaks in an unknown tongue," says Parham, "the other students can see the cloven tongue of fire descend upon the speaker."

Parham asserts that the students--all Americans without education in foreign languages--have lately spoken in French, German, Swedish, Bohemian, Chinese, Japanese, Hungarian, Bulgarian, Russian, Italian, Spanish and Norwegian; or Norse.

"We have received several messages to go into all the world and preach the gospel," said he, "and we must obey the command. A part of our labor will be to teach the churches the uselessness of spending years of time preparing missionaries for work in foreign lands when all they have to do is to ask God for power and then have faith that the power will come."

"All things come though faith," Mr. Parham continued. "We ask God for food and raiment and we receive them. I have started out many a day without a cent and returned with $25; my prayers had been answered. There was nothing supernatural about it. I needed the money for the Lord's work; He knew it, and put it into the hearts of men who had money to supply my wants. I needed a turkey for my students on Christmas; I prayed for it; my prayer was answered; a farmer's wife sent us a turkey. We wanted power from on high to help save the world; we prayed for it; we received it."

Stone's Folly, where the Parham school is conducted, was built several years ago by an eccentric old man named Stone. He never lived in it, and the property was unoccupied until Parham leased it. The house cost $40,000. It is built on the order of an old feudal castle, three full stories, with thirty rooms. The drawing room is used by the students for a chapel. A tower which commands a fine view of the city and surrounding country is known as the praying tower. Prayer in the tower is continuous night and day, the students relieving each other.

While Parham and half a dozen of his band are in Kansas City teaching the new doctrine, thirty or more students are at Stone's Folly, praying for them.

This article appeared in the **Topeka Mail and Breeze** *on February 22, 1901.*

• • • • • • • • • • •

WARSAW, MISSOURI

No doubt the **Nazarene** readers are wondering concerning our whereabouts. We closed our successful meeting at Elk Falls two weeks ago. We held but two and one-half weeks, but in that time about 70 professed pardon or purity. We organized a County Holiness Association and believe it is on good footing.

People came from miles around. Many calls came from the surrounding country but owning to weariness of mind and body we postponed all for the present. Receiving an invitation to visit our holiness band here, we came. We stopped over twenty-four hours in Topeka, arriving there the Fourth of July. By request we preached in a tent that night and next day visited Rev. C. Parham's Bethel College. Great excitement has lately been aroused concerning this man and his followers who claim to have received the "gift of tongues." We found the famous "Stone Mansion" as it was formerly known, and were treated in a very courteous manner by Rev. Parham.

The "Stone Mansion" now known as Bethel College, is said to be the result of a wild investment of $47,000.00 by a man who afterward died in poverty. Never have we entered a grander palace built for private use. The woodwork alone cost $7,000.00.

A special meeting of the students was called for our benefit and they were requested to speak, which accordingly they did, in languages foreign to us and themselves. It is claimed they have been understood by people of many different languages. As Rev. Parham drove us down to the city, he told us how marvelously God provided. The students gathered on the veranda and sang, "God be with you," as we rolled away. When I told Bro. Parham the reports I heard concerning his means for conducting the work, he laughed heartily. In his own peculiar way, and said, "I have only thirty-five cents I can call mine and just enough for supper."

We find our holiness band here very much alive though persecuted by church members and ministers. We go for a camping out next week.

In Jesus Name,
Herbert and Lillie Buffum

*This article was published in the **Nazarene Messenger** on July 18, 1901. In the years to come, many holiness people recieved the Pentecostal message, including entire denominations, others, however, refused to accept tongues as the initial evidence and became extremely adversarial.*

Charles F. Parham's pulpit shaped grave stone in
Baxter Springs, Kansas
(Photo by Larry Martin)

Chapter 9

JOY AND SORROW AT BETHEL

By Sarah E. Parham

I do not want to repeat, but I wish to say that I was an eyewitness to what has already been told, and thank God for the blessed experience He gave us at Bethel, the baptism of the Holy Spirit. As we were gathered together in an upper room, in one accord, truly "God came down our souls to greet, while glory crowned the mercy seat." It is better felt than told, for only those who have had the same experience can know the joy we felt at that time. If you would like to know what we received, read Acts 2, which tells you of the outpouring of the Holy Spirit just as He came to us, manifesting His presence by speaking in other tongues.

While two or three were speaking in other tongues, as the Spirit gave utterance, I thought perhaps they were going as missionaries to foreign fields, and did not know whether this wonderful experience could be for me, I felt so empty and unworthy. I knelt down and prayed, "Lord if this is for me, I want it." My desire was to have all that had been purchased for me at so great a cost on Calvary. Jesus said, "It is expedient for you that I go away, if I go not away the Comforter will not come, but if I depart I will send Him unto you" (John 16:7). Though so unworthy, my heart longed for God's best, the fullness of His love, manifest in my life, and I prayed, "Lord, I want all there is for me." The glory of God filled my soul, I found myself repeating this prayer, and then began speaking, in tongues.

How glad we were when Mr. Parham returned from his meeting in Topeka and received the baptism of the Holy Spirit also. When at last we retired for the night, he said I talked in tongues in my sleep, still praising God.

The following days were mostly spent in prayer and thanksgiving. Our favorite songs, which we never tired of singing were "All Hail the Power of Jesus Name," and "The Comforter Has Come." Concerning these first days of the outpouring at Topeka, it was soon noised abroad that Pentecost was being repeated and shortly afterwards an article appeared in the Topeka paper ridiculing the speaking in tongues. Other newspapers began to hear it and send reporters, and articles appeared in the Kansas City and St. Louis papers concerning the outpouring. This advertised the work and letters came pouring into the school asking for explanations, and some came to see what the Lord had done.

One day my dear aunt came, who had always been like a mother to me. How glad we were to see her, also surprised as she always had told us when she was coming. After we had talked awhile she said, with a sigh of relief, "Well, you seem to be like you always were." We then understood, she had seen the newspaper reports, and fearing we might be losing our minds, had come to look after the children.

We had known great joy and now we were to know great sorrow. Our beautiful baby boy, now a year old, whose big brown eyes seemed always to be looking with a gentle longing into the future, was taken very sick. He had never been sick before and we hardly realized how sick he was until March 16, 1901, he was gone. His loving gentle nature, ever ready to confide in all, had won the love of the school. It seemed impossible for us to give him up. Some of the students said, "Come let us all pray, God can raise the dead. Surely He will bring him back to life." But as I looked at his little face so pure and innocent, I felt that it would be a selfish prayer to try to call him back to a world of sin and sorrow. As God had seen best to take him, we must learn to say, "Thy will be done."

Yet how hard it is sometimes to leave it all with God without questioning why? Had it been a lack of faith on our part, or was it to test our faith to see if we would go on and preach the gospel of healing? You who have had like experience know how many questions will fill our minds and we often, perhaps unjustly, condemn ourselves. If we could always see and understand our sorrows and trials there would be no test of faith. We should be walking by sight, instead of walking by faith.

As parents our little children often ask us "Why?" but we do not always explain things to them, as they could not understand. So when Peter questioned Christ, "What will this man do?" Christ only answered, "What is that to thee, Follow thou me."

The sun that hardens clay, will also melt the wax. Sorrow will either harden our hearts or melt them. If we rebel against God's will, our hearts will be hardened, but if we yield to His will, He will tenderly draw us closer to Himself. Oh, may we yield our lives to Him and let sorrow soften our hearts as wax, that He can mold and fashion us according to His good pleasure, that we may be made all glorious within. That we may shine as gold, tried in the fire, until we reflect His likeness.

I wandered away from the house to pray, out on the beautiful lawn so fresh and green in the beauty of spring. Lost in my own sorrow, I did not at first notice that someone else had come out there for the same purpose. He was a guest at the school, highly respected by all, but so quiet and reserved that we did not know his hidden sorrow. When he saw me, he came to me and expressed his sympathy. "Yet," he said, "your sorrow is not as hard to bear as mine. Yours is a dead sorrow, with no stain of sin, mine is a living sorrow." He then told me his story. His wife had left him, his home was broken up, his life ruined.

How sad, I could not think of a word of comfort, but oh, how many broken hearts there are in this world, carrying a "living sorrow," trying to hide it with a smile, or bury it with worldly pleasures. A few unkind words may break the tender cord of human affection and thoughtless deeds end in a tragedy. How careful we should be each day to say or do nothing that we might have cause to regret. Yet those too, who bear the "living sorrows" may take them to the Living Christ, the Man of sorrows, the Great High Priest who can be touched with the feeling of our infirmities for He knows "the flesh is weak."

As I returned to the house, Mr. Parham met me with a bouquet of flowers in his hand. I knew he felt the loss as keenly as I did, yet he tried to be brave for my sake. He gave me the flowers saying, "These are not for little Charlie, they are for you." How often I have thought of this. Kind words and flowers can not help the dead, but how much comfort they may sometimes bring to the living. Though the flowers soon fade, how long sometimes, they will remain fresh in the memory, and the loving thought of the one who gave them.

We went by train to Tonganoxie, Kansas where we were to bury our baby. Mr. Parham was very patient with me, reminding me that I had yet much to live for as he pointed to our two children, Claude and Esther, sitting side by side in the seat before us, looking sad, though unable to understand it all. Sometimes our minds are so centered on our sorrows and lows, that our eyes are blinded to the blessings and loved ones who are still ours. Everyone was very kind to us, yet we could feel that some of our friends, who did not believe in healing, were hoping now that we would give up this belief.

Could we give it up? No. If our faith was in what we could see in the natural, truly our faith might now be shattered, but our faith had been established in the Word of God. As we had seen healing and salvation so closely connected in the atonement, we felt to give up our faith in healing, we would lose our hope in salvation and all was lost.

If part of the Bible is false, it is all untrue, or else it is all true. God's Word is true, even though seemingly we had failed and been defeated. Yet perhaps it was not defeat. God's infinite plan might have been carried out, though we could not understand it with our finite minds.

We returned to Topeka and continued the work at the Bible school, but before the summer was over the beautiful building was bought to be used as a pleasure resort. We had dreamed that the building had been bought and that it burned to the ground. Mr. Parham told the men, and warned then that if they used the building (that God had honored with His presence) for ungodly purposes, they would not prosper. They may have thought we told them this with a selfish motive but this was not so.

We believed nothing could come to us except as God permitted. If we had to give up the building, the purpose of the school must have been accomplished. We were willing to go elsewhere as He might direct. The building was bought and the students went to different places, some of them remaining with us in Topeka where we rented a building for a short time.

While there a lady from California visited us. She was hungry for the baptism of the Holy Spirit. We tried to explain it to her but she seemed unable to grasp the truth.

She wrote us, that after she got home her heart was still longing for more of God. She prayed, "Lord, even though I don't understand, give me what they received on the day of Pentecost," and she began to speak in other tongues. How glad and encouraged we were to get her testimony.

We then left Topeka, Kansas, and went to Kansas City, Missouri.

*This chapter is an abbreviation of "Joy and Sorrow at Bethel," a chapter in **The Life of Charles F. Parham: Founder of the Apostolic Faith Movement** written by Sarah E. Parham.*

Epilogue

THE END OF STONE'S MANSION

FOLLY IS BURNED
FAMOUS STONE MANSION GOES UP IN SMOKE.
FIRE BREAKS OUT THIS FORENOON FROM
UNKNOWN CAUSE.
USED AS ROAD HOUSE.
RECENTLY HAS BEEN NOTORIOUS AS
HARRY CROFT'S PLACE.
MUCH OF THE FURNITURE WAS SAVED BY
NEIGHBORS

"Stone's Folly," known as Harry Croft's road house, one mile west of Washburn college, was totally destroyed by fire this morning at 11 o'clock. The origin of the fire is unknown.

"Stone's Folly" is the name applied to the mansion built at a cost of about $40,000 in boom days by a wealthy Englishman named Stone. It was acquired by the American Bible Society on a mortgage, and was early this spring sold to Harry Croft and turned into a road house. It has figured conspicuously in a number of raids.

The fire was first discovered by Mrs. Croft and another woman, who were in the building alone. It started in a room over the kitchen in the northwest portion of the building, which was two stories high.

When Mrs. Croft discovered the flames she became frightened and ran two blocks to the residence of Robert Stone, where she found W.A. Frazier, a brother of Mrs. Stone, working in the yard. He together with Henry Barker, a brother-in-law of Robert Stone, hastened to the building.

"The first thing we attempted to do," said W.A. Frazier to a reporter for the **State Journal**, "was to send in the alarm to the city fire department. We could hardly find the telephone. Mrs. Croft was so frenzied she was nearly out of her mind, and could tell us nothing. We found the telephone, however and sent the alarm.

"Next we hurried to the room on the upper floor, where the flames were beginning to spread, and closed the doors, thereby confining the flames to the room for a time.

"We succeeded in carrying all the furniture from the rooms on the first floor and two rooms on the second floor from the house before the flames gained such headway that we were compelled to desist.

"The chemical engine from the fire department reached the scene of the fire too late. The building was still in flames but was too nearly destroyed to save any portion of it.

"The chemicals were turned on the fire for a few minutes, but it did no good."

A considerable portion of the furniture was removed from the house a few weeks ago and stored in the city.

The building was insured for $5,000. The loss will greatly exceed the amount of the insurance.

The building was called "Stone's Folly" because the man who built it shattered his fortune in erecting it. It was a veritable place and was one of the most expensive buildings in or near Topeka.

This article was originally published in the **Topeka State Journal** *on December 6, 1901.*

• • • • • • • • • •

THE LAST OF STONE'S FOLLY
COSTLY MANSION USED AS ROAD HOUSE BURNED
OCCUPIED BY CROFTS
NOTHING SAVED OF THE ONCE
FINE RESIDENCE
MODELED AFTER MEDIEVAL CASTLES--
AMERICAN BIBLE SOCIETY OWNED
$7,000.00 MORTGAGE

Yesterday saw the passing of the old "Stone's Folly." This building which stood a mile or more west of Washburn college, was entirely consumed by a fire which originated in the woodwork adjoining a defective flue, about 10:30 A.M. yesterday and gained an impetus that placed it completely beyond the control of the men who tried to save the building.

A chemical engine in charge of Firemen Pyle and Sovereign was sent out from the fire department headquarters, but the men were unable to do more than prevent the outbuildings from catching fire. The total loss can hardly be estimated as the value of the property had depreciated greatly during recent years. It was purchased last summer for $7,000 by Harry and J.B. Croft, who had paid but $1,100 upon their investment. Insurance for $5,000 was held in favor of the American Bible Society, the mortgagee of the property.

"Stone's Folly" has lately become better known as Croft's road house. Harry Croft, who used to be known in Topeka as a jointist, purchased the place on the 20th of last July and opened a resort. He has since been arrested by the county authorities once or twice and recently gave out that he had quit the business of selling liquor. His wife and mother-in-law were the only regular tenants of the large house, which had eighteen furnished rooms. Mrs. Croft was the first to notice the fire, which was already under strong headway in a northwest room of the second floor. She called the neighbors, who gave all assistance in their power. The furniture in the lower floor and in one of the second story rooms, about $300 worth in all, was saved. The Crofts estimate their actual loss at about $1,800.

In 1887 or 1888, E. R. Stone, who had made considerable money in the boom of Topeka real estate built a mansion, modeled after the medieval castles he had seen in Europe. It was placed a mile and a half west of Washburn college. Its grounds covered ten acres planted in evergreens and fruit trees. No one seems to know exactly how much was spent upon the building the reports vary from $20,000 to $60,000. The lower figure is probably the most accurate. The interior was finished throughout, no two rooms being trimmed with the same variety of wood. Mahogany, rosewood, magnolia, walnut, black and white, curly pine, birdseye maple, butternut and oak from all parts of the country are said to have been used in the inside decorations.

Outside, the house was striking in appearance. It was of three-stories, surmounted with towers and battlement. The walls were of heavy studding with a brick veneer and stone cornices. Now the large foundation, forty by seventy-five feet, running from east to west, lies full of discolored bricks. No part of the wall is left standing; a dismantled chimney stone projects twenty-five feet above the ruins.

Mr. Stone could not keep the pace he had set and when the boom broke was forced to part with his pretentious dwelling. Some say that he was defrauded out of his property, and that the man who did it is in the penitentiary, but that story is not verified. He himself never told how much the house cost, but the sum was a large one.

After the Stone family left it, several tenants tried to occupy the place, but it was too large for the use of an ordinary family and was finally closed up. A year ago last fall, the Parham School of Tongues procured the building, which was then owned by the American Bible Society. The School of Tongues which was conducted by Charles F. Parham, was composed of a sect of fanatics who believed they could acquire the use of all languages through faith alone. Thirty or forty of the faithful lived in the building and were supported by charity.

They were in possession of the place when the Crofts purchased. The School of Tongues has moved to Kansas City.

This article was originally published in the **Topeka Daily Capital** *on December 7, 1901.*

Front View: Stone's Mansion
From **A Voice Crying in the Wilderness**
(Public Domain)

Side View: Stone's Mansion
Sketch from the **Kansas City Times**
January 27, 1901
(Public Domain)

The Tower of Prayer at Stone's Mansion
Sketch from the **Kansas City Times**
January 27, 1901
(Public Domain)

A List of Illustrations

About the Author

Dr. Larry Martin is an evangelist, traveling through-out the United States and 24 countries of the world. His life was dramatically changed in 1996 after a unexpected en-counter with God's glory. Martin traded dead religion for a living relationship with Christ and denominational politics for power with God. His only remaining ambition is to be part of the last days revival that is sweeping the world.

Prior to entering the evangelistic ministry, Martin was the President of Messenger College in Joplin, Missouri. He also served the college as the Dean of the School of Lifelong Learning and as a professor of theology and mis-sions. Before coming to Messenger College, Martin spent more than twenty years pastoring churches in Oklahoma, Texas and Tennessee.

While an ordained minister with the Pentecostal Church of God, Martin was a member of the denomination's Curriculum Commission, Strategy 2000 Steering Committee and General Board. He also served on the District Boards of three states. Although it was once an important part of his life, Martin no longer covets de-nominational affiliation or recognition.

Martin is a graduate of Cameron University, Oklahoma Missionary Baptist College, Southwestern Oklahoma State University and The Assemblies of God Theological Seminary. He also earned the Doctor of Ministry degree at Austin Presbyterian Theological Seminary in Austin, Texas.

Also a free-lance writer, Martin's articles have appeared in *Ministries Today, The Missionary Voice, The International Pentecostal Holiness Advocate, The Pentecostal Messenger, The Pentecostal Minister, The Message of the Open Bible, The Pentecostal Leader, The Church Herald and Holiness Banner* and *The Church of God Evangel.*

In addition to **The Topeka Outpouring of 1901**, Martin has written or edited **In the Beginning, For Sale: The Soul of a Nation**, and **The Complete Azusa Street Library**. He has also contributed to several other works.

Martin is married to Tajuana Jo and they have two children, Matthew Dallas and Summer Jo. They reside in Joplin, Missouri.

For information on Dr. Martin's schedule or a catalog of other books on Pentecostal\Charismatic history, including
The Complete Azusa Street Library,
please write:

Christian Life Books
P.O. Box 2152
Joplin, Missouri 64803